Everything on the Line

Ellis Amdur, M.A., N.C.C., C.M.H.S.

Calming and De-escalation of Aggressive and
Mentally Ill Individuals on the Phone

A Comprehensive Guidebook for

Emergency Dispatch (9-1-1) Centers

An Edgework Book
www.edgework.info

Notes and Notices

Everything on the Line: Calming and De-escalation of Aggressive and Mentally Ill Individuals on the Phone

By Ellis Amdur, M.A., N.C.C., C.M.H.S. © 2011

ISBN: 978-1-950678-01-3

A Message to Our Readers

Edgework is committed to offering the best of our years of experience and study in the interest of professional and public safety. We ask that you express your respect for these intentions and honor our work by adhering strictly to the copyright protection notice you'll find below. By choosing NOT to reproduce these materials, you're supporting our work and making it possible for us to continue to develop materials that will enhance the safety of both the professionals for whom this book is written and the public. We thank you sincerely for your vigilance in respecting our rights!

Notice of Rights

Limited Liability and Disclaimer

Credits

Photographs by: Dreamstime.com
Illustrations by: Shoko Zama
Design: Soundview Design Studio

Contents

Books by the Author (and Co-Author)

Published by Edgework www.edgework.info

On the De-escalation of Aggression

CHAOS TO COMPLIANCE: Communication, Control, and De-escalation of Mentally Ill, Emotionally Disturbed and Aggressive Offenders
A Comprehensive Guidebook for Parole and Probation Officers
Ellis Amdur & Alan Pelton

EVERYTHING ON THE LINE: Calming and De-escalation of Aggressive and Mentally Ill Individuals on the Phone
A Comprehensive Guidebook for Emergency Dispatch (9-1-1) Centers
Ellis Amdur

GUARDING THE GATES: Calming, Control and De-escalation of Mentally Ill, Emotionally Disturbed and Aggressive Individuals
A Comprehensive Guidebook for Security Guards
Ellis Amdur & William Cooper

GRACE UNDER FIRE: Skills to Calm and De-escalate Aggressive and Mentally Ill Individuals in Outpatient Settings: 2ⁿᵈ Edition
A Comprehensive Guidebook for Health and Social Services Agencies, and Individual Practitioners
Ellis Amdur

IN THE EYE OF THE HURRICANE: Skills to Calm and De-escalate Aggressive and Mentally Ill Family Members: 2nd Edition
Ellis Amdur

SAFE BEHIND BARS: Communication, Control, and De-escalation of Mentally Ill and Aggressive Inmates
A Comprehensive Guidebook for Correctional Officers in Jail Settings
Ellis Amdur & Chris De Villeneuve

SAFE BEHIND THE WALLS: Communication, Control, and De-escalation of Mentally Ill and Aggressive Inmates
A Comprehensive Guidebook for Correctional Officers in Prison Settings
Ellis Amdur & George Galaza

SAFE HAVEN: Skills to Calm and De-escalate Aggressive and Mentally Ill Individuals: 2nd Edition
A Comprehensive Guidebook for Personnel Working in Hospital and Residential Settings
Ellis Amdur

SAFETY AT WORK: Skills to Calm and De-escalate Aggressive and Mentally Ill Individuals
A Comprehensive Guidebook for Corporate Security Managers, Human Resources Staff, Loss Prevention Specialists, Executive Protection, and others involved in Threat Management Professions
Ellis Amdur & William Cooper

THE THIN BLUE LIFELINE: Verbal De-escalation of Mentally Ill and Emotionally Disturbed People
A Comprehensive Guidebook for Law Enforcement Officers
Ellis Amdur & John Hutchings

On Martial Arts

DUELING WITH OSENSEI: Grappling with the Myth of the Warrior Sage
Ellis Amdur

HIDDEN IN PLAIN SIGHT: Tracing the Roots of Ueshiba Morihei's Power
Ellis Amdur

OLD SCHOOL: Essays on Japanese Martial Traditions
Ellis Amdur

In Gratitude for Expert Critique

The following professionals have vetted this book. With each draft, I corrected errors of fact, added new information, and fine-tuned the manuscript. I then submitted it to the next expert. I have appreciated the direct criticism—one of the qualities of a good emergency call-taker is the understanding that the task supersedes protecting someone's feelings.

All responsibility for this book, however, must lie in my hands. Any errors, in particular, are my responsibility. Given that lives are on the line in work such as this, please don't hesitate to contact me if you believe that any part of this book is inaccurate or needs additional material. I will revise the book, as needed in future editions.

Pamela Cooper has 25-years in her public safety career as a trainer and front-line 9-1-1 dispatcher.

Kelly Sharp is the owner of Workplace Consulting NW LLC, with the following degrees and certification: B.A. in Communication, M.A. in Education. She has a 25-year career as a trainer for both military and law enforcement agencies, as well as a 15-year career as a training officer, dispatcher and call-taker in a 9-1-1 center.

Wendy Thompson has served 19 years with the Guelph Police Service (Guelph, Ontario, Canada) as a 9-1-1 Dispatcher and 15 years as a Tactical Scribe Liaison for the Canadian Critical Incident Inc., and Tactical Scribe instructor.

Deanna Wells is manager for the dispatch center in Cowlitz County, Washington State, and has been in the business for about 20-years. She is also part of a multi-disciplinary team that discusses issues such as mentally ill callers.

Gailyn Williams is currently communications officer, Long Beach Police Department. Has over 10 years career as dispatcher, as well as a communications officer with a focus on crisis management, liaison, and negotiations.

Laurie Brown was first hired as an entry-level dispatcher in 1980. She is currently assistant director of Santa Clara County's 9-1-1 system. Ms. Brown also holds an A.S. and B.S. in Management, and an M.S. in Emergency Services Administration.

Who This Book Is For

This book, part of a series on interaction with people in extreme states, represents my life's work on communication with mentally ill people, and the verbal de-escalation of aggression. Each book contains the same core information, tailor-made to specific professions or situations. This volume concerns call-takers and dispatchers in emergency dispatch centers (9-1-1 in the United States), whose function is to rapidly assess whether a crisis exists, and if so, whether it requires the dispatch of police, fire fighters, or emergency medical personnel.

In many agencies, the call-taker is responsible for processing calls received directly from the public, some of which are emergent. The dispatcher has a number of executive functions including notifying the proper emergency responders to go to the scene of the crisis situation. In other agencies, the call-taker and dispatch functions are folded into one. The call-taker is further responsible for on-line crisis intervention, either while emergency responders are en route, or if, due to any one of a number of reasons, he/she is the only one with access to the reporting party. In much of this book, I will use the title "dispatcher" when referring to either call-taker or dispatch functions, although I will use call-taker when I am exclusively referring to direct service with the public.

Figure 1 One Veteran Dispatcher's Distinction Between Call-takers and Dispatchers

A dispatcher and a call receiver may be two different types of people, although some people are effective in both roles. Great dispatchers anticipate what questions to ask and what is needed to help the emergency responders do their job and stay safe. They are always one step ahead of the next request, and are able to visualize the scene. They aren't afraid to question the responder, asking such a question as "Do you need me to do this or that?" Furthermore, they are proactive, offering back ground information on the person the responders are about to contact, history of incidents related to the subject, and their mode of operation (MO).

The dispatcher is generally aware of other contacts or incidents the subject may have been involved in because they work for all police or fire agencies countywide, while the emergency responder's knowledge is often limited to events that occurred within his/her own agency, not adjacent police or fire agencies.

Figure 1 (continued) What a Call-taker Must Do

A call-taker on the other hand must have good customer service skills, a clear vision of their responsibilities, good report writing skills, and an art for interrogating callers. They must be able to differentiate between an immediate crisis, and larger issues that would interfere with the caller's ability to either remain safe or move towards safety. We don't want a call-taker telling a caller to go outside and see what is going on if it's not safe for them. We don't want to tell the caller to run out of a burning house, if they have to run through a burning living room to do so. We want to help a caller escape an attack, but we don't want to tell them to try and leave the home if the perpetrator might be waiting outside. We want call-takers who can think outside the box, and can multi-task as well. We need people who can ask:

- "What is this person telling me?"
- "What do I hear in the back ground?"
- "Is what I'm hearing making sense?"
- "Do I need to ask more questions?"
- "What will the responders need to know when they pull up to the scene?"
- "Is this a medical emergency?"
- "Will my EMS responders be safe?"
- "Do I need to send police?"
- "Do I need to ask more scene safety questions?"

Like the dispatcher, the call-taker must be able to visualize the scene. At the same time, the call-taker must not embellish information. If the caller didn't state it, don't make assumptions and add it to the call. The call-taker must be a good report writer, because they (and others) must be able to distinguish in their text what the caller told them, and what the call-taker thinks is going on.

The behaviors of mentally ill individuals can be quite bizarre and hard to understand. What we can't understand is unpredictable, and therefore seems to be dangerous. By learning the meaning of behaviors exhibited by mentally ill, agitated, and aggressive callers you will become more skillful in assessing if such an individual is truly dangerous. In many situations, you will also have the ability to calm them. Often, you will find that your presence, conveyed through your voice, prevents a situation from escalating.

It is my hope that this book, which encompasses over 25 years of experience in face-to-face and on-the-phone encounters with mentally ill and emotionally disturbed individuals, augmented by the expert consultation of a number of veteran call-takers and dispatchers, will be invaluable in readying both newer call-takers and experienced veterans for such calls. This book is part of a series of guidebooks for people who must face aggressive individuals. Other books in this series are specific to those who work as police officers, probation and parole officers, corporate security professionals, emergency medical technicians, and for those who work in corrections institutions, inpatient hospital units, and social services positions. I have also written a separate version for families who live with mentally ill family members. Please refer to the website **www.edgework.info** for more information on all of these books, as well as information regarding training on the same subjects.

Introduction

Imagine an individual, perhaps a child, slipping off the bank of a flooding river. They are smashed by the waves into the rocks and water begins to fill their lungs. Then their hand touches a rope, a single line among all the confusing tendrils of branches, vines and muck in the water. They grab hold, and are pulled upwards towards a point of light. They emerge into the air, gasping, and soon, helping arms are reaching for them and pulling them from the water. No help would ever have arrived, however, if not for that single strand, that one cord within the chaos that links the victim to rescuers.

That one cord referred to above is the role of the emergency dispatch center. But dispatch, linking the helpers to those who need assistance, isn't their only role. In many cases, a call-taker actually manages the crisis at a distance—telling the victim what to do to stay safe, or to go towards safety. In other events, the call-taker's voice alone keeps that person from slipping away into despair or even unconsciousness. Returning to our image, let us imagine that the drowning individual believes that the rope you have thrown to them is a viper—only the power of your spirit, conveyed through your voice—will lead that person to take hold.

Not all calls are heroic, however. Many callers are people lost in mental illness, and others are embittered by events in their lives, often unasked for and undeserved. Other people are simply selfish—that such a service as yours exists means to them that they are entitled to use it. They make demands, vent complaints, or simply spew venom. Such calls take their toll. It isn't easy to determine if a crisis exists, so you must stay on the line, suffering the verbal abuse. Those who misuse the emergency system rarely face consequences, and they call again and again, leading the call-taker to ever increasing levels of frustration or even burn-out—a kind of slow-motion post traumatic stress when one becomes blunted and indifferent to others, even those genuinely in need.

We must also consider our own role in difficulties that can occur with callers. If we bring our own problems to the worksite, and allow them to seep into our interactions, situations that could otherwise be managed spiral out of control. Thus, the heart of de-escalation and control of crisis situations requires the de-escalation and control of ourselves.

The primary aim of this book is to augment your abilities in dealing with people suffering from serious mental illness. I will attempt to highlight anything that an emergency dispatch center can do that will lead to a safe resolution with these most puzzling of callers. A second goal is to provide information that may aid you in the recognition of dangerous and manipulative callers, as well as honing your ability to de-escalate and control them. In essence, this book focuses on the art of taking chaos, the substance of all too many calls, and coalescing it into an ordered system centered on your voice.

SECTION I

Essentials of Crisis Communication
With Agitated, Aggressive, or
Mentally Ill Individuals

CHAPTER 1

Core Skills

The Essentials

Success at managing disorderly or aggressive callers is enhanced by a number of factors. Some of these are as follows:

They include the five W's—**Where, What, Who, When, and Weapons:**

- **Where.** Get the location of where the incident is happening, and get them to tell you again! Absolutely nothing can be accomplished if emergency responders can't reach the caller. Given that cell phones are increasingly replacing landlines, call-takers must ask for the address and make sure that they've got it right. Remember, the same street and number may exist in two adjacent towns, miles apart.

Figure 1.1 One Dispatcher States

"Getting the location correct is the most important responsibility. Never assume. The biggest emotional pain that I have experienced is when I got the location incorrect. What people do to one another is tragic, but making a mistake on the location is worse for the call center."

- **What.** Always ensure that you know what is going on. And don't assume that the first thing the person tells you is the real story! There was a recent incident in Vancouver, Washington, which was, by report, a hostage situation—as it turned out, the "hostage" was working with the alleged "hostage taker" to draw police into the line of fire. As long as you have phone contact, continue to gather information, even when you are sure you understand the situation.
- **Who.** Be sure to find out who is involved: those presenting a threat, those who are injured, victims, and others on the scene. As obvious as this statement may be, the irrational or confusing verbiage of mentally ill, confused, agitated or drug intoxicated individuals can cause call-takers to miss essential data.
- **When.** When did the crisis happen: recently, currently, or is it about to happen?
- **Weapons.** We must do everything necessary and possible to keep our police officers, firefighters, and EMTs safe. Questions about weapons and their locations, a history of violence, past or current threats to responders, drug or alcohol use, and any other potential dangers must be answered as fully as humanly possible.

Other basic requirements are listed below:

- **<u>Follow standard procedures.</u>** Given the fluid nature of human relationships, you will never be limited in your opportunities for creativity. Nonetheless, there MUST be standardized procedures for dealing with potentially or actually aggressive individuals—as well as those who are mentally ill. It is true that one sometimes has to make an exception and go outside the rules, but you must understand that, in doing so, you are taking personal rather than institutional responsibility for your actions as well as exposing yourself to personal liability. It may be the right thing to do, but you will have to prove it—not only by positive results, but also by your explanation. In any event, this must be the most unusual of occasions.

- **<u>Adaptability.</u>** Notwithstanding the necessity for a predictable environment with standardized procedures, dispatchers and call-takers must also be flexible. Staffing constraints, other logistic problems, and callers who, for a number of reasons, are disruptive to the dispatch center or the equilibrium of a call-taker, require everyone to be creative. Standardization must never become rigidity.

- **<u>Solid boundaries.</u>** Callers need to know (or learn) what kind of behavior isn't allowed. The following will be helpful in maintaining ethical standards:
  a. The call center must be known as an institution where staff is vigilant in maintaining ethical and moral relationships in interactions with callers.
  b. Unless it is an emergency call where you are required to stay on the line, the dispatcher should be empowered to advise callers who use abusive language that they must clean up their language. The exception is a working felony, where putting up with offensive language becomes secondary to officer and public safety.
  c. All employees in the call center must ensure that interactions among staff are professional—staff members won't act in any way among themselves that negatively impacts the care of callers.

Figure 1.2 Example From a Veteran Dispatcher

"Over the past 19 years I have witnessed and have been on the receiving end of bad behavior in several call centers. Rather than intervene and help while the event is in progress, some staff sit back and allow their co-worker to fail or make a mistake, then point out the mistake to others or supervision after the fact. This impacts the safety of responders, citizens, and the reputation of your communication center."

- **<u>Customer service.</u>** Treat people how you would want your own family to be treated.

Figure 1.3 How One Veteran Call-taker Puts It

"Remember, we are the 'first responder.' We set the mood and greatly impact the outcome of the experience and relationship the citizen and responders have with 9-1-1."

- **Integrity**. Above all, be yourself—this should be your greatest strength, but that is only true when you offer the best of you to your profession. Without this, all the de-escalation methods in the world are just empty words.
- **Intuition.** It is a truism that the other senses of the blind—hearing, smell, and touch—are far more sensitive than those of sighted individuals. A call-taker begins to develop similar sensitivity. There is a "sixth sense" as well called intuition. This is the ability to become aware of small changes in the tone of voice, pattern of speech, or background noises that indicate that something else beyond what is said on the phone is happening. If your intuition conflicts with the answers you've been given, ask the same questions in different ways, looking for inconsistencies.
- **Empathy and visualization.** Empathy doesn't mean to "feel sorry for someone." That is sympathy. Empathy is the ability to put yourself in another's place, to get a sense of what they are feeling or experiencing from the sound of their voice, and in face-to-face contact, their facial expressions and body language. The best call-takers have an ability to get a "felt sense" that something is wrong from the slightest of clues. He/she has the skill to know what is going on at the other end of the line, and visualize it as if it is right in front of them.

CHAPTER 2

Threat Assessment

Areas of Concern for a Phone Threat Assessment

The information in this chapter isn't offered as a checklist that you tick off, item by item, with each caller. Instead, the information should serve as "red flags." Some of this information will be derived from answers to questions that the caller gives you—others will be behaviors they manifest during the phone call. If, for example, the caller complains about being beaten as a child, there is a flag flying—this person may be very reactive or belligerent to authority, or have a hidden goal of taking revenge on people who are more powerful.

All information has a context. For example, you may become aware that a caller owns several guns. Certainly, that is a risk factor to emergency responders in and of itself. The fact of gun ownership, in itself, isn't enough information. More than half the citizens in the United States own guns. You need to know why they own weapons, how the guns are used and in what context, and what the weapons mean to them.

Such a list isn't an absolute predictor of aggression or violence. Nonetheless, if you are aware of the information below, you will have a much better idea who and what to watch out for. **This is the kind of information that, if known, can save the lives of the emergency personnel that you dispatch.**

- **<u>A past history of violence, including bullying and intimidation.</u>** This is one of the most important factors. Violence is a learned behavior, which becomes easier to use as a problem-solving strategy each time it is used. Furthermore, it is rewarding—some people feel most powerful when they are violent.
- **<u>Possession of weapons, fascination with weapons, and a past history of using weapons</u>**. In particular, we must be concerned when the person has a history of brandishing or using a weapon, talking about a weapon in menacing terms, or fantasizing in a pathological manner.
- **<u>History of being a victim of physical abuse or witnessing physical abuse and violence.</u>** Particularly significant is to have witnessed abuse of a family member. The victim of abuse often hates his own weakness and begins hating weakness in others as well. Once this occurs, it is a natural move for some people to begin victimizing what they hate—the weak.
- **<u>Head injury or dementia.</u>** These are associated with impulse control problems.
- **<u>Fear of attack.</u>** Fearful people often lash out in defensive violence.
- **<u>Poor impulse control and low frustration tolerance.</u>** Inability or unwillingness to tolerate limit setting. "I want what I want and I want it now and you'd better not keep me from it."
- **<u>Recent stressors and losses.</u>** Such as bereavement, separation, and divorce can make one more willing to become violent. One also feels that one has nothing left to lose.

- **A feeling of victimization and grievance.** Every problem is ALWAYS someone else's fault.
- **Use of intoxicating substances.** Almost all intoxicating substances tend to dissolve the internal barriers that hold us back from our base desires, among them aggression.
- **Physical pain or discomfort (chronic pain especially).** These include medication side-effects or withdrawal from drugs. People who hurt are irritable, as if to say, "There's got to be someone at fault for me feeling so miserable."
- **The individual who has already "given up".** They expect interaction to be difficult or negative. Their response can be, "What the hell—nothing will help. If I'm aggressive, I matter—at least I can make my mark on the world—or on you."
- **Severe psychopathological symptoms:**
  a. **Rapid mood swings.** Such a person is unpredictable, and can suddenly flare into rage just when the responder thinks he/she has solved the problem.
  b. **Hallucinations, command hallucinations.** A person may be hearing voices that are telling them to do something terrible. If you think someone is hearing voices, ask what they are hearing.
  c. **Mania.** This is a state of excitement, typified by rapid speech, grandiose thinking, very poor judgment, and impulsive behavior. It is a behavior we see in people with bipolar disorder (manic-depression) or intoxication on methamphetamine or cocaine. One sign of this is extreme boisterousness or markedly loud, self-centered happiness.
- **Interactional factors between the aggressor and victim.** Particularly in domestic violence situations, the aggressor views the victim as being inflexible or controlling, or denying the aggressor his/her due. In short, the aggressor usually believes he/she is the victim. They will view emergency responders as further victimizing them.
- **Religious and cultural clashes.** We must be aware that different religions and cultures sanction violence according to different values. This isn't only true for cultures of nations or ethnic groups. For example, street-gang culture regards humiliation (being "dissed") as the worst possible experience and sanctions violence on the part of the humiliated person. Let me be quite clear that I'm not calling for any accommodation on the part of a 9-1-1 call-taker regarding divergent cultural rules. However, if a caller gives an indicator that they or someone else intends to be violent, knowledge of the cultural ideology that might drive that violence gives the call-taker something to discuss when communicating with the caller as well as information to pass on to the first-responders.
- **Post Traumatic Stress Disorder (PTSD).** When in a panic engendered by PTSD, the brain believes that one is in a survival situation. Survival demands simplicity, therefore, the only options the brain in survival mode offers are fight, flight, freeze, or faint. Obviously, "fight" in this case, means that the person believes they must fight for their life. PTSD is often evoked during certain holidays associated with loud, popping noises such as the fourth of July or Memorial Day. Even more central are any events that evoke memories, or worse, re-experiencing the traumatic event. Smells, more than any other sense, seem to be tied directly to memory and hence, are particularly likely to evoke such an episode.

- **History of prior arrests.** This presents with a number of risk factors as listed below:
  a. The person may have resentment towards authority, blaming them for what they perceive as unjust treatment.
  b. They may be afraid of being arrested again, and thus, more willing to fight to resist this.
  c. They are very possibly rule-breakers.
  d. Even if their arrests were for non-violent crime, they may have experienced and been trained towards violence during their incarceration.

The Art of Threat Assessment

The following are information that might be relevant in specific situations. The more personal information you acquire about the caller, the safer emergency responders will be. A call-taker should try to get such information about the caller, the subject of the call and any witnesses.

- Although you will always try to get the callers full name and date of birth, this is particularly important when your caller seems to be mentally ill. In addition to criminal records, there may be very important information in their files in hospitals and mental health agencies. Furthermore, asking demographic information can sometimes be an effective way of assisting a panic-stricken or agitated person to calm down. The attention required to give "vital statistics" helps people order their thoughts. *If they have a military history, vital information, otherwise not recorded, can be secured by the police of the Department of Veterans Affairs.*
- Listen for background noises, i.e., passing trains, whistling of tug-boats, etc., to ascertain a possible location for patrolling officers to locate the troubled subject.
- Occasionally, the caller, particularly one in an abusive situation, will be afraid to give their address or other identifying information, and as noted earlier, if they've called on a cell phone, you won't know where they are unless they tell you. They desperately want intervention, but at the same time are terrified that their abuser will find out that they called. A good first step is to say, "We need to send officers to help you now, please tell me where you are…." But sometimes, particularly with a child or terrified person, they won't give you their location. In such a case, don't argue with them to get the address information right away. Ask other questions to flesh out the situation. As they talk with you, and answer your questions, they will begin to trust you and thus, a few minutes later, when you ask again, they may be willing to tell you where they are located.
- Ask for a description of the problem: then ask further questions to understand the context.
- Ask open-ended questions, not leading questions: For example, don't ask, "Was he white?" Instead ask, "What race was he?" Don't ask, "Did he have a beard?" Ask, "Did he have any facial hair?"
- Always try to ascertain if the individual or anyone else involved in the crisis is currently using or has recently used drugs or alcohol. This includes prescription medication.
- If there is any sense of chaos, violence, or danger, ask if anyone has been hurt. If so, ask how and get specific. In some situations, try to speak to others in the house to get a general picture from each person what is going on. If you are on the phone with a child and it is safe to do so, try to remain on the phone with them. Kids are literal and generally don't lie. As a call-taker, you have to think about prosecution in many calls, and the honest statements of a child on 9-1-1 audio are very powerful in trial.

> **Figure 2 CAUTION**
> If you ask a child or cognitively-impaired individual if they feel "safe," they might answer in the affirmative because they feel safe now while talking to you. You need to ask further questions to find out if a potential aggressor is nearby or soon returning and if the person will continue to feel safe once the phone call is terminated.

Core Questions Regarding Potential Violence

Situations will arise requiring you to remain on the phone with a caller for an extended period of time. Even though emergency response personnel are on their way, the person may be barricaded, or otherwise not immediately accessible upon their arrival. Given your responsibility to do whatever you can to try to ensure responders' safety, you must try to gather information regarding the caller's potential for violence. Ask direct questions in a powerful, yet calm manner. You are striving to demonstrate that you are able to handle anything they might mention, even angry or threatening statements. Reminder: the quality of their answer such as tone of voice, when they pause, what they skip over, what they reference in an oblique rather than direct way. The quality of their answer such as tone of voice, when they pause, what they skip over, what they reference in an oblique rather than direct way is as important, or more so, than the specific answer they give. In asking questions the following will be helpful:

- Ask direct questions to ascertain if there is any threat of violence or suicide. For this reason, ask questions so that the person has to elaborate, rather than asking "yes" or "no" questions. For example, "So he hit you? Did he use a weapon or just a part of his body? Was his hand open or closed?"
- Always ask if the person has access to weapons, particularly if an emergency response is being considered.
- Ask if other people in the location have weapons as well.
- Some people get remarkably overly specific in crisis situations. For example, without any intention of being dishonest, they will truthfully inform you that *they* don't have a weapon, but not mention, unless asked, that their brother is armed with a knife at all times.
- Others have their own personal definition of a weapon, only including, for example, a gun. A knife, on the other hand, is a tool. Ask if they or anyone else has ever used any object to hurt other people or to defend themselves.
- Ask if anyone has made such statements, as "They won't take me alive," or "I'm not going back to jail."

In more extended phone contacts, questions beyond the basics can include the ones listed below. (NOTE: This isn't a complete list. These examples are to help you understand the scope and nature of the questions you need to ask.):

- "Have you hit someone in the last six months?" "How about the last year"? "Have you ever been arrested for assault?" "How about for fighting with someone?" Notice the nuanced levels of the questions. You are able, here, to assess their familiarity with the legal system (what if they deny assault, but confirm an arrest for "fighting.) By asking "six months," you may get a more manipulative person, who otherwise might lie, to say, "Not in six months," because they think that's all you care about.

- "Tell me what happened today?" The context of why callers were assaultive, what it meant to them, why they thought they had no other options, and why they might have chosen violence first, not last. All of this is vital information.
- "I'm just asking a question to understand where you are at. I also want to make sure that you are treated with respect. What kind of thing might someone say that might make you mad?"
- "When you get mad at someone, what do you do? How do you handle it?"

SECTION II

Centering: Standing With
Strength and Grace in
Crisis Situations

CHAPTER 3

Introduction to Centering

The Kind of Problems that Knock Us Off Center

Dispatchers work in a challenging, sometimes chaotic environment and often have no control over many aspects of the job. They must follow the policies of their own agency as well as those of the agencies they serve. Everything is recorded, documented, and by law kept for various periods of time, available for public scrutiny through the Freedom of Information Act. The level of responsibility, liability, and accountability is enormous. There is little room for error, yet the public expects perfection.

The typical dispatcher is meticulous and detail oriented, taking pride in his/her work and enjoying intrinsic satisfaction performing a thankless job. Most seasoned employees at call centers develop a "thick skin" and are able to distance themselves from other people's problems. If you didn't have this talent going into the job, you certainly acquired it if you continued. Not surprisingly, "dark humor" is a common way to de-stress over an incident. Although outsiders and family members may not understand, this macabre sense of humor displays an understanding of the limits of what one can do and what is out of our control.

The two greatest reasons for stress are personal failures, and not knowing what has happened after emergency responders went out. Personal failure distresses even the most seasoned dispatcher. Knowing you didn't read a situation right, missed something, or said the wrong thing causes emotional anguish and can even damage your health. Then there are those calls where you do everything right, but this is cold comfort when the outcome is negative.

Figure 3.1 Concerning the Issue of Not Knowing the Result

One veteran dispatcher says: "I worked in a big city emergency call center. The goal was to take 50 calls in an hour. That average was disrupted when a working felony occurred and you needed to stay with the caller until the police had the situation under control. With those high numbers, I was haunted many times wondering about the outcomes of many of the calls. The police have the luxury of finishing the callout versus the call-taker who has gone on to take hundreds of more calls before the officer ever clears the scene."

Finally, everyone of us has different vulnerabilities—different types of callers who can throw us off center.

Figure 3.2 Examples of the kind of calls that throw us off center

- Ariana is a teenager with a heartbreaking life of abuse. When things aren't going well in her life, she phones the emergency call center making suicidal threats. Emergency response must be dispatched to her residence. Unlike many such callers, she is always respectful, and in a way, that makes things harder. She never acts in a way that allows one to achieve emotional distance from her. Due to the fact that she has made several serious suicide attempts, out of emotional pain that might break any one of us, some staff experience immense pressure each time she calls, feeling personally responsible about whether Ariana lives or dies.

- Maria, one of the dispatchers, is simply tired. It isn't one particular caller who has thrown her off center; it is the job itself. She is tired of the emergency calls, the constant demands for information updates from police and fire departments, tired of having to respond to the misery of many people, particularly as she thinks that her own life isn't something to brag about. As days and weeks pass, she becomes more and more distant—her voice is now as flat as glass. She speaks in a monotone. She rarely talks to the other dispatchers whom she used to consider good friends. She sleeps poorly, and on days off, finds nothing regenerates her. Instead, she sits, watching TV or eating snacks she has no hunger for. The weekend ends, and another round of callers appears. She begins to view them with contempt, thinking, "This will never end." They simply live to breed and call and mess up their lives—nothing else."

- Sometimes, one's own personal history can affect one's response to a call. Joanne married young, at age seventeen, and survived seven terrible years of abuse. She managed to escape, raising two children on her own. Eventually, she got a job as a call-taker. She answers a call from a young woman in almost exactly the same situation as she was in twenty years before. She handles the call perfectly, but afterwards, begins shaking and can't stop. Her husband was never prosecuted, and she can't stop thinking that he could find her any time he wants, and maybe this time, she won't be able to escape.

The Danger of Burn-out—When the Pathological Becomes Normal

Emergency call-takers are engaged in ongoing threat assessment. Some professionals become so familiar with pathology that the abnormal becomes normal. The dispatcher no longer reacts in a natural way.

Figure 3.3 When the Abnormal Becomes Normal (Hypothetical example)
Leo has a diagnosis of schizophrenia. He is a drain on both emergency response personnels' time and on the dispatchers' forbearance because he rambles on about delusional fears. He had already cost the taxpayers well over ten thousand dollars in response to his calls. He has been prosecuted for false reporting on two occasions, but released based on a court decision that he has diminished capacity and has no awareness that he is doing wrong. He has also been committed to a mental hospital on numerous occasions, but he compensates well on his medications every time and is released, at which point he immediately goes off his meds, and lapses back to the same condition. There is no legal way to require him to be on his medications. Some dispatchers are absolutely burned out on him, and wish, at minimum, that he would take a long course of "bus therapy" to somewhere far away. One evening, he called, in his typical rambling way, mumbling about vultures hovering over blood on the ground, and glittering knives in the sky, very similar to calls he'd made in the past. The dispatcher repeatedly asked if the caller was witnessing a crime. He replied that it was a vision. The call-taker terminated the call, after listening, irritably for a few minutes. In fact, Leo was witnessing a violent assault outside his window. Because police didn't respond until another person called, five minutes later, the victim was fatally injured.

Other dispatchers become burned out at the human misery to which they must respond, coupled with the sometimes abrupt demands of emergency personnel who "need answers now." The burned out dispatcher literally doesn't "want to hear anymore." Such a staff person misses vital information, the subtle hints that indicate that, even though the caller is odd, obnoxious, or a poor informant, an emergency is, in fact, occurring. Additionally, burnout is a kind of "slow motion post traumatic stress." Every day the body is flooded with stress hormones. The burned-out individual can begin to overeat, experience sleep disturbance, or other disruptions of mood and temper, and eventually, serious health problems.

We humans aren't made to live in perpetual crisis, even if it is others' crises to which we are responding. Trying to deal with people with mental illness, personality disorder, hysteria, anger, and other chaotic emotions is particularly debilitating. It is even more harrowing when, on occasion, you realize that your reactions to that caller seemed to make things worse. Perhaps things have gotten so bad that you have lost confidence in your abilities or pride in the work you do, yet it would be economic suicide to quit the job. You have to work, and yet the work is tearing you down.

For some dispatchers, it isn't even crises calls that take the life out of the job. Many people in our society have assumed an attitude of complete entitlement, demanding "service" from emergency response as if we are hired help, calling to complain.

- "I need a cop to find my keys."
- "My nine-year old won't get out of bed for school."
- "The three-year old neighbor has a stick."

- "I need a ride to the store."
- "I didn't get enough sauce on my pizza and I'm really mad."

One might write a book, called, "Gimme," composed solely of such 9-1-1 calls. You know, however, that you have no control over others. You may wish for them to act a certain way, you may even demand it—but ultimately, it will be their choice whether they do what you desire. If you are working this job, you will get the entitled selfish stupid calls, the heartbreaking tragedies that you hear happening in real time, just out of reach, and the unanswered questions, such as "What happened to that call?" That's what you signed on for and that's what you will receive in full measure.

Nonetheless, we aren't powerless. The easiest way to change the quality of any relationship—and this applies equally to a professional at a dispatch center as any other locale—is to change yourself.

This section will offer you specific strategies to change how you "organize" yourself in relation to your callers (and honestly, to other people as well). These strategies revolve around maintaining self-control. When we read the word control, many of us imagine something forceful and rigid. Such dispatchers and call-takers exist. They, the over-controlled, over-controlling staff, are among the least effective personnel in a call center. Contrary to such rigidity, we aim to develop the ability to adapt to circumstances in a powerful, fluid, and purposeful way. Sometimes you quietly listen, and other times you quickly intervene. At each and every moment, you are prepared to take a stand, assert yourself, or when the situation requires, take over completely. You aren't defensive or on your guard. Rather, like a cat walking along a fence, you are at ease, yet ready for anything that comes.

CHAPTER 4

The Power of Gravity—
I Have All the Time I Need

When your callers are in crisis, they believe that there is no time and no hope of solving the problem. If you also believe that, you will be unable to help because you, too, are in crisis. You must instill in the caller a belief that you know what you are doing. You must display an attitude that, no matter what, you have all the time you need to find an answer to their problem. Whether the other person agrees or not isn't the question. The answer must start within you. This is true regardless of the number of calls that you are expected to answer in an hour or the ticking clock or chime that indicates that calls are backing up. **This is an attitude, not how many seconds are on the clock.** It is when we accept the other person's sense of time rather than ours that we lose control of the situation.

Figure 4.1 Author's Experience

Many years ago, I was working on a crisis line, and the first call I ever took started with, "I've got a gun to my head and you have ten seconds to tell me whether I should live or die." First day, first call. I whirled around for my supervisor for back-up, and she was consulting on another call. After a couple second's silence, I said, "Wow. I gotta tell you something. I'm in graduate school. Man's search for meaning, life-and-death, all that? But I'm just reading about it. You are living it right now! Man, we have GOT to talk!" He replied, "We do?" And I had him hooked.

There are some times when the situation is so terrible, and happening so fast that it seems inconceivable that there is enough time. With this attitude I am talking about, however, time "slows down," and yet, you move both faster and more efficiently.

Figure 4.2 Different People Have Different Ways of Finding Gravity

One veteran dispatcher states: "At the risk of sounding too spiritual I have often asked God to "handle this one,— that I will be his conduit of words." **Another dispatcher says**: "I don't have any illusions—all I have is the power of my words. So I concentrate on making every word powerful. If this takes time, so be it. Better a few powerful words than useless jabber."

CHAPTER 5

A Fair Witness

There is nothing lonelier than a sense of helplessness or shame, feelings frequently evoked when one experiences physical or emotional attack. This is especially the case when a caller—someone to whom you have pledged to help—is aggressive, ungrateful, or abusive. In such situations, the harshness of the world can seem to roll over your life, indifferent to whether you do well or poorly, even live or die.

Emergency dispatchers have a particular dilemma. Some of the things that affect you most are so ugly or appalling that, were you to discuss them with a partner or other family member, you would, in effect, be inviting violence or obscenity into your homes. There are many times when you should speak of what you went through to loved ones, at least when they are both willing to hear you out and stand-up enough to *be able* to hear you. Still, there are many other occasions when it is a mark of courage and decency to forebear passing on that burden.

Therefore, we must cultivate peer support. This can include strategizing sessions or co-supervision, but there are times that this is the last thing we need. Instead, we need someone to simply bear witness, and demonstrate by their presence that we are still a part of the human family, despite the sense of isolation engendered by being in a terrible situation. A **fair witness** is someone who knows you, who respects you, and who is willing to hear you out. Lest there be any mistake, this isn't always a solemn occasion—sometimes, you and the person you are talking with will be using outrageous humor. At the same time, such humor can sometimes be a screen to get us past something we should really be talking about in more depth. When you are a fair witness for another, you must be able to differentiate between the times that laughter truly is the best medicine and those times when they need to speak about what is behind the laughter. Conversely, you must be able to ask the same from your own fair witnesses—for example: "No, Tommy, you have to hear me out. This one isn't sitting well with me. I don't need advice and I don't need jokes right now. This is what happened…."

Keep Contact with the Outside ("Real") World

Many dispatchers, sharing such intense experiences in a closed environment, can get cut off from those not part of the emergency world. This can really skew your perception of reality. Remember, most of the world isn't in crisis! Keeping contact with people not part of the crisis system and sharing such things as hobbies, sports, and conversation is another kind of "fair witnessing." People in the "real" world bear witness that the entire world isn't one of chaos, violence, or illness.

Imagine that the only thing you have to drink is coffee—strong, bitter, and black. It certainly energizes you, but after too many cups, you get that metallic, coffee taste on your tongue. Now imagine going to a well and getting a cup of pure spring water—that is the outside world. We need to regularly go to the well if we are going to keep ourselves healthy.

CHAPTER 6

It's Not Personal
Unless You Make It So

Rule 1: If It's Not About Survival, You Don't Have to Win

A desire to win is associated with primitive mental processes linked to dominance hierarchies. Rather than striving for the truth or for a fair exchange, we end up striving to overwhelm the other. Unless you are in a struggle for your own or someone else's life, <u>you don't have to win</u>. Your goal is to establish a line of communication with enough clarity and peace that you can get the information you need to make a safe resolution most likely.

Rule 2: You Don't Have to Give Back What You Get

We believe ourselves justified when counter-attacking, because they "hurt us first." A defensive reaction or move toward pay-back is, however, an attempt to assert dominance over the other. When you are offended because of what they say or do, remember that <u>it is the act of a professional not to respond in kind</u>.

Rule 3: It's Not Personal

Although their attacks might seem directed at you, they <u>aren't personal</u> unless you make them so. If they are untrue, what is there to be upset about? And if they are true, then you are reacting in anger when someone tells you the truth and no matter how ugly the presentation, the truth is something to be faced and accepted rather than fought in anger.

On those rare occasions when the caller somehow gets to you and pushes your buttons and you feel like you've lost control over the call, remember you have a button of your own—the "Hold Button." You work as a team, therefore, ask one of your team members to take over the call when you just can't get centered with a particular caller.

Rule 4: Ears Open

When you react emotionally, it is very possible that you won't be aware of signs of danger. You have a responsibility to pick up any warning signs that could indicate that the emergency response personnel are at risk. If you are busy with your hurt feelings or anger, you will surely miss something. Some of the items you might miss are listed below:

- Is the person's aggressiveness escalating? If so, what is the proximate cause of their escalation, and what type of aggression are they moving into? (See the latter sections of this book.)
- Are there any indications that there are other people on scene who may present a risk to emergency response personnel?

- What are your emotions? Are you getting mad too? If so, is this contributing to a situation that would result in others getting hurt, either by provoking further escalation from the caller, or because, in your anger, you aren't fully paying attention to what they are saying or not saying? Never allow yourself to be lowered to the level of an aggressive or abusive caller. Never allow anyone to rob you of your excellence.

CHAPTER 7

No Caller Will "Own" Me

Aggressive individuals, particularly those with a mental illness or personality disorder, can be infuriating. Using desperate survival strategies that include paranoid blaming, passive-aggressive foot-dragging, manipulation, or mean-spirited attack, they may hone in on your weak spots in a form of verbal violence. They know, or soon find out, what your hot buttons are.

The trouble with the ideas in the last chapter on "not making it personal" is that such rules work fine until our buttons are pushed. Then, pain or anger clenches inside us like a fist. In these moments, we are likely to violate our own professional standards. Although it is certainly true that you can and should cut off an abusive call when it is clearly not an emergency, you don't have this luxury when there is a felony in progress, or when you must keep the caller on the line until you can complete an adequate threat assessment.

Why does verbal abuse affect us?

The brain is an organ of survival. Thus, it is organized to respond to threat. We are aware of danger through physically-based pattern-recognition, a rapid response of the more primitive areas of the brain. A large object moving rapidly towards us, a sudden pain, or a violent grab initiates a cascade of responses—fight/flight/freeze/faint—that are geared to keep us alive in the worst of circumstances. At lower levels of danger, particularly that presented by another human being, we are provoked into posturing—displays of dominance/submission—which serve to maintain or enhance our position in a social structure.

The curse of being human is that these survival responses are precipitated by physiological cues, especially those that shock or surprise us. When our guard is down, and someone verbally assaults us or unexpectedly violates our sense of right and wrong, we physically react in the same way that we do when under life-threatening attack, even though survival isn't truly an issue. Someone can call you the ugliest name in your world, sneer, deride, or demean you, but they present no danger at all. The only real danger would be if, in response, you lose control of your own actions. When our buttons are pushed, we react as if we are threatened with bodily harm and this reaction, in most cases, ill-serves us at establishing control over a dangerous situation. It is important, therefore, to look deeply within yourself and identify what your buttons are. Buttons come in four primary colors (with lots of possible combinations):

- *You've challenged what I love.* Someone attacks the things we love or treasure and drags them through the muck.
- *You've pointed out a truth I hate.* Someone points the truth out to us—the things we are insecure about or don't want to face.

- *You've violated what's right.* Someone says something that violates our deepest sense of right and morality.
- *You've challenged my authority,* or acted in such a way that I feel you have power over me.

Bracketing

Sometimes, we can roll with insults by taking a deep breath and speaking in slow and measured tones. However, this is sometimes not enough, particularly if a caller hits one of those hot buttons. Beyond knowing what to do or say "in the moment," the real solution comes through a kind of "inoculation"— a tool to make you immune to people trying to get to your hot buttons. This is a technique called *bracketing*. It means facing your vulnerabilities head on, and taking action so that no one can use them against you.

For some of you, a fair witness could be of great assistance in helping you to stay truthful and strong. Talking about such difficult issues with another person, however, often leads others to respond with reassurance, reframing the "bad" as "good," or offering amateur counseling of one kind or another to make the vulnerabilities disappear. Developing a truly strong mind requires you to face the worst head-on without the refuge of a comforting friend or witness.

Here's a worksheet that can help you name and bracket your own hot buttons. It isn't necessary that you make a complete list of every statement that could push your buttons. I am simply trying to get you thinking and you can add to this list at any time.[1]

- I can't stand it when someone attacks or demeans <   >, because that's something I love and treasure.
- I feel outraged when someone demeans <   > because it is something I believe to be unquestionably right and good.
- People get me defensive when they say or point out <   >, because, to tell the truth, I hate it in myself (or, it is a flaw....).
- When people say or do <   >, I lose it because it's as if they are taking control of me, or disrespecting me.
- They better not say <   >. That's the one word I won't take from anyone.

What sets you off?

Statement	Why?
EXAMPLE: When people say or do < >, I lose it	It's as if they are taking control of me, or disrespecting me.

Daily Inventory

We are most likely to lose our temper when we are blind-sided—not expecting an attack. As previously stated, sudden emotional shock elicits the same responses in the nervous system as a physical threat. For example, if a friend unexpectedly insults your race, religion, or gender, it is very likely that you will shift into a response using the parts of your brain that express raw emotions. This part of the brain, the limbic system, is no longer concerned about the truth, about negotiation, or how to make peace. Instead, it views the world as one at war, and perceives the other person as trying to usurp your position of strength. When off-guard, we are in the most danger of flaring up and losing our "temper," a term from metallurgy meaning *our flexibility, our edge, and our strength.*

Therefore, to create a mind prepared for the worst, we must "take inventory." Every morning upon waking, every shift when you first sit down to work at the dispatch center, and every night when you go to sleep, you simply run an inventory—as if flipping through a deck of cards—to remind yourself of each of your emotional triggers. By bringing them to consciousness, you prepare yourself for the possibility that someone will accidentally or deliberately push one of your buttons.

If you have to walk across a narrow beam, something you have practiced a number of times, your body will be relaxed, but not stupidly so. Because of your "skill at-ease," you can make micro-adjustments in your balance and gait if a breeze shifts the beam, or if you are momentarily distracted by someone's voice. Similarly, if you have taken emotional inventory, you are unsurprised when a person tries to push one of your buttons. I don't mean that you are at hair-trigger readiness, a state closer to paranoia; instead you develop a sense of spaciousness so that when someone tries to push one of your buttons, you can deal with it effectively rather than reacting as if you are under attack. You will find it easier to take control of a critical situation, and much easier to emotionally disengage afterwards.

When you really know your buttons, you can't be surprised any longer when those ugly things are being said. You can't be blindsided. In essence, your insecurities are still there and so are your weaknesses, but you have control over them. You say, in essence, "Yes, I am that. But no one will ever be able to use it against me."

CHAPTER 8

Circular Breathing—
Be the Eye in the Center
of the Hurricane

Aggression and violence can smash through a previously peaceful day with the suddenness and force of a hurricane. Chaos doesn't only take over the day, but also it may overtake you. However, when you can respond by stepping coolly into the worst of situations, you embody the eye of the hurricane, with all the chaos coalescing and revolving around you. The root of this skill lies in breath control. Using a method called "circular breathing," where you breathe slowly, with focused attention, you regain control of your physical self. When you control your body, you control your life. Then you are in a position to take control of the crisis as well as the person causing it.

Figure 8.1 A Clarification from the Author

Lest there be any confusion—This isn't a "time-out" where you take a few deep breaths and then return to the subject, refreshed. That is ridiculous. You can be moving very fast while breathing very slowly. You are training your body and mind to go into this breathing as a response to danger and stress. It is a trained response that should be instantaneous.

As someone who has practiced the following technique for over 30 years, I can assert that it has become automatic. Unlike my younger days when the adrenalin would hit and I'd start breathing fast and high in the chest, my breathing usually slows down in emergency situations. You are practicing to develop a "pseudo-instinct"—trained response so bone-deep that you don't even have to think about it, anymore than you have to tell yourself to yank your hand from a hot stove.

Two Variations

Circular breathing is derived from East Asian martial traditions and was used to keep warriors calm on the battlefield. There are two variations. Try both, alternating between them, until you know which one works best for you. From that point on, exclusively practice the one you prefer. *If you train regularly, it will kick in automatically, rather than being something you must think about.* In essence, your breath itself becomes your center, not your body posture, not the situation in which you find yourself, or whatever is going on between you and the aggressor.

Circular Breathing Method #1 – Initial Practice Method

- Sit comfortably, feet on the floor, hands in your lap.
- Sit relaxed, but upright. Don't slump or twist your posture.
- Keep your eyes open. (**As you practice, so you will do.** If you practice with your eyes closed, your newly trained nervous system will send an impulse to close your eyes in emergency situations. If you want to use a breathing method for closed-eye guided imagery or relaxation, to get *away* from your problems, so to speak, use another method altogether.)
- Breathe in through the nose.
- Imagine the air traveling in a line down the front of your body to a point two inches below the navel.
- Momentarily pause, letting the breath remain in a dynamic equilibrium.
- As you exhale, imagine the air looping around your lower body, between your legs and up through the base of your spine.
- Continue to exhale, imagine the air going up your spine and around your head and then out of your nose.

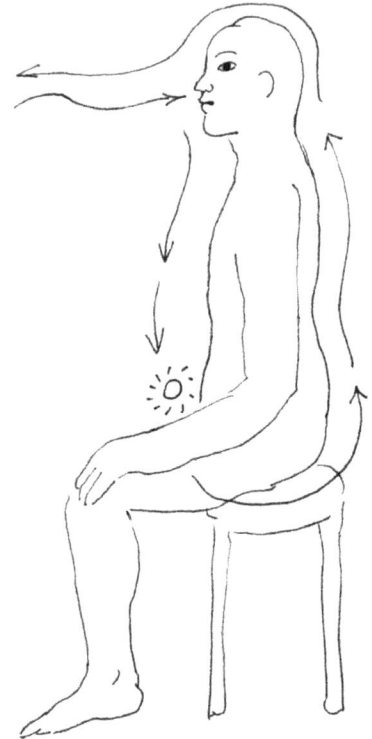

Circular Breathing Method #2 - Initial Practice Method

- Sit comfortably, feet on the floor, hands in your lap.
- Sit relaxed, but upright. Don't slump or twist your posture
- Keep your eyes open. (**As you practice, so you will do.** If you practice with your eyes closed, your newly trained nervous system will send an impulse to close your eyes in emergency situations. If you want to use a breathing method for closed-eye guided imagery or relaxation, to get *away* from your problems, so to speak, use another method altogether.)
- Breathe in through the nose.
- Imagine the air going up around your head, looping down the back, falling down each vertebra, continuing down past the base of the spine to the perineum, and looping again, this time up the front of the body to a point two inches below the navel.
- Momentarily pause, letting the breath remain in a dynamic equilibrium.
- As you exhale, imagine the air ascending up the centerline of your body and out your nose.

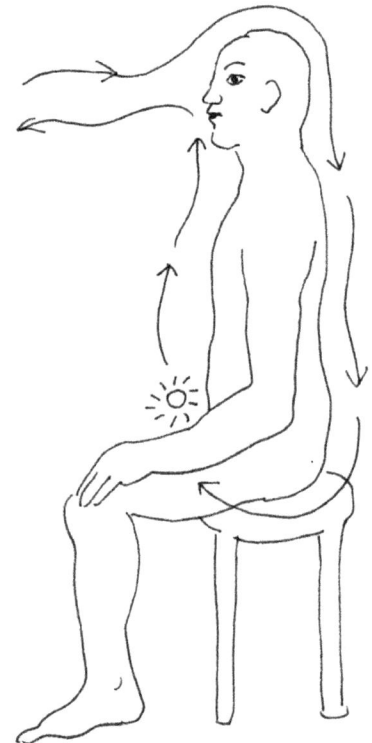

How to Practice Circular Breathing

Some people find that imagining their breath has light or color is helpful. Others take a finger or object to trace a line down and around the centerline of the body to help focus their attention. Again, choose which of the variations works better for you.

When you first practice, do so while seated and balanced. Once you develop some skill, try circular breathing standing, leaning, or even while driving. Most people find that after a short period of time they don't need to visualize the circulation of the breath. You literally will feel it, a ring of energy running through your body. You will begin to feel balanced and ready for anything.

Once you are comfortable with your chosen pattern of breathing, experiment with it in slightly stressful circumstances, like being caught in traffic, or sitting through a meeting as a supervisor drones on about new paperwork requirements. When you can better manage yourself in these slightly aggravating or anxiety-provoking situations, you are ready to use it in an emergency situation. If you have practiced enough, you will naturally shift into this mode of breathing when the crisis hits. There will no longer be a need to tell yourself to "do" circular breathing. It will become reflexive, automatic, replacing old patterns of breathing that actually increased anxiety or anger within you.

Remember, this is a skill to be used during emergencies, not for relaxation or meditative purposes. Instead, you are trying to enhance that ability to do whatever is needed to fight, to dodge, to leave, to think gracefully and intelligently—whatever is required for the situation at hand.

When to Use Circular Breathing

The way you organize physically affects your thinking. For example, if you assumed the posture and breathing of a depressed person (slumped body, shallow breathing, sighing), and maintained it awhile, you would actually start to feel depressed. Similarly, if you clenched your fists, and start glaring around with a lot of tension in your body, you will start to feel angry. (You have probably observed people working themselves up from anger through rage into an attack in just this way.) Similarly, circular breathing creates its own mindset: one adaptable and ready for anything, equally prepared for an easy conversation and for a fight, yet fixed on neither.

This method of breathing is very helpful when you are anticipating a potentially dangerous or upsetting situation, anything from being told to take over a call with a panic-stricken child in danger to a follow-up contact with an unfortunately belligerent first responder. This breathing activates the entire nervous system in a way that enhances both creativity and the ability to survive.

Even in the middle of a confrontation, particularly a verbal one, there are many times when this breathing will have a very powerful effect. Not only do we get more stressed or upset in the presence of an upset person, but also we become more peaceful in the presence of a calm one. People tend to template their mood to the most powerful individual close by. You surely know call-takers who often calm a situation down the moment they pick up the phone and speak one phrase. You have probably seen the opposite as well. Using this breathing method is a vital tool in making you the former type, a man or woman of quiet power.

Use this method of breathing after the crisis as well. You will need to regroup to go on with the rest of your shift. Circular breathing will bring you back to a calm and relaxed state, prepared to handle the next crisis, should one occur.

If we bring feelings from a crisis situation back home, we carry that crisis back to our family. Therefore, before entering your home, sit quietly in your car or even in the yard, and practice this breathing for a moment or two. The only thing that should come home is "you," not the stressful calls that you handled that day.

Figure 8.2 Comment From a Veteran Dispatcher Regarding Breathing—The Spiritual Level

When breathing in this manner during a call where a person has been killed or seriously injured while on the phone with the dispatcher, she states, "Time slows down. It is as if things are happening in slow motion. It's like being in a different dimension for a time. During these horrible events, maintaining my breathing, I have felt the presence of God many times.

Circular Breathing to Ward Off or Even Heal From Trauma

Figure 8.3 Note on Circular Breathing

Although the material in this section may seem a little to "therapy" oriented, it is invaluable if you ever find yourself having difficulty dealing with a traumatic reaction and, for one reason or another, help is either not available, or you can't or shouldn't avail yourself of the help that is offered. Keep this in reserve for those times when you need it.

Post-Traumatic Stress Disorder (PTSD) isn't defined by how horrible the event sounds in description. It is defined by the victim's response to the event. PTSD isn't exactly a problem of memory. It is a problem because the event hasn't fully become a memory; it is still primarily experienced as if it is happening right now. When an event is fully a memory, it is experienced as something in the past, over and done with. Another way to think of it is as a scar; it may not be pretty, and it certainly is a signpost that something significant happened to the person, but it no longer hurts. A trauma, on the other hand, is an open-wound. It is an *experience*. It isn't in the past, and in fact, may be affecting every moment of the person's life, or emerge suddenly, when evoked by something that elicits a sense that the event is happening again.

In PTSD, the person's nervous system is set to react as if there is an emergency whenever the trauma is recalled. This can be anything from an explicit memory to a small reminder: for example, although he doesn't consciously know why, a soldier gets anxious every time someone coughs, because one of his squad coughed right before a bomb went off. Because trauma affects the brain at the deepest levels associated with survival, logical interventions (anything from reassurance to cognitive therapy) offer only equivocal success in helping people emerge from trauma. Image-associated breathing techniques, which affect the brain as a whole, can assist people in realizing that the event is over and no longer a part of present experience. The following should be helpful in handing PTSD:

- Let us imagine that something very upsetting has happened to you. Perhaps you even recall an old trauma that still plagues your mind.

- Whenever you think about it (or it forcibly intrudes into your consciousness), your body tenses or twists in various ways. Your breathing pattern often changes.

- If this is your situation, go someplace where you won't be disturbed for a while. Make the mental image of that trauma as vivid as you can tolerate. This takes some courage, because most of us simultaneously avoid-as-we remember. Rather, if only for a moment or two, meet it head on and re-experience it. If you physically organize (with your breath, muscular tension, posture, etc.) *as if* something is happening, the brain believes that it truly is occurring right now. Notice, in fine detail, how you physically and emotionally react. As difficult as this may be, it is important to establish for yourself what your baseline response is to the trauma. You must clearly experience what it "does" to you when you recollect it.

- Now take a couple of deep sighs. Sighing breaks up patterns of muscular tension and respiration. This is like rebooting your computer when the program is corrupt.

- Mentally say to the ugly experience: "Hush. You move right over there to my right (or left). I'll get to you in a minute." For some people, it is even helpful to make a physical gesture, "guiding" or "pushing" the experience off to the side. You won't be able to *force* yourself to stop thinking about an experience if it has psychological power. Instead, move it aside, as if you are guiding a wounded person to a waiting room while you organize yourself to properly deal with it.

- Now initiate your preferred method of circular breathing.

- As the memory creeps back in (and it will), just breathe and center yourself, again placing the memory off to the side. Once again say, "Hush, I'll get to you in a minute." You can't fight it, so don't try. Just ease it aside until you are ready.

- When your breathing is smooth and your body is centered, you will be relaxed like an athlete, ready to move but with no wasted effort.

- Now, deliberately bring that ugly memory or trauma into your thoughts and imagination. Now, as you find yourself reacting, continue circular breathing, trying to bring yourself back to physical balance as you focus on the traumatic memory.

- Bit by bit, in either one session or a few, you will notice that you are increasingly able to hold the image with a relaxed body and a balanced posture. You are now able to re-experience the memory without the same painful, tense, or distorted response you had in the past. You are, metaphorically speaking, turning the open wound into scar tissue.

Think of how you hold babies so that they are safe—you don't drop or squeeze them so tightly that they are frightened or uncomfortable. To be strong in the face of trauma is very similar in that you internally hold the memory with all the grace and strength with which you hold babies so that they are safe, whether asleep or struggling to see over your shoulder. You aren't wiping the slate of memory clean. Rather, you are placing it in a proper context—something that happened to you, but doesn't define you.

CHAPTER 9

The Intoxication and Joy
of Righteous Anger

It would be naïve, indeed, to assume that anger is noxious for all of us. There is a subset of people who don't mind arguing or even fighting; at least when they believe their cause is just. Such individuals go off-center in an interesting way—they get happy when someone offends them. They get a smile, perhaps, and mentally say, "If you want trouble, you've come to the right place."

Figure 9.1 A Supervisor's description of a combative call-taker

Consider someone at my call center. She is an excellent radio dispatcher, well-respected by her peers and the field units, able to calmly handle any crisis. Her sense of humor is legend; she can be droll or pleasurably sarcastic but always maintains her professionalism and never crosses the "appropriateness" line. Then she gets on the phone with an uncooperative caller and suddenly the whole room can hear her. She is loud, abrasive, demeaning, and demanding. She isn't having a conversation; she is conducting an inquisition. Everyone's response is, "Oh that's just Molly" as they wince and wonder how she gets away with this behavior.

When functioning in a professional capacity, such people have an especially difficult task—they must recognize that when they feel *good*, they are in danger of becoming part of the problem. Instead of imposing calm on a situation, they escalate it, and don't mind in the least. They define the person they are dealing with as the aggressor, and then they feel completely righteous in responding in kind. One might think that such an attitude is confined to face-to-face encounters, but it can also occur on the phone. A caller makes racist or sexist remarks, or laughingly describes what it is like to hurt a child. Yet another caller is demanding, blaming, and provocative. In any of these cases, the call-taker, rather than calming himself/herself, feels justifiably angered, and is happy to respond in kind. This can lead to unprofessional responses, not only to a caller, but also to an emergency responder—a police officer or EMT. Circular breathing (Chapter 8) is actually difficult for people who go into righteous anger because they don't *feel* that there is a problem. Your task, if this description fits you, is to recognize the special joy that comes with righteous anger, and act to center yourself to a calm state of mind, rather than the excitement or joy of righteous anger.

Figure 9.2 A Note on Righteous Anger

Supervisors will have a difficult time explaining how counterproductive such righteous anger is, because the "happy warrior" feels justified. Supervision should be framed in terms of staying calm as a means to control the other person. In other words, when the call-taker gets angry, whatever the reason, the provocateur has taken control of the situation.

SECTION III

Dealing With People With
Unusual, Intense, and Eccentric
Communication Styles

CHAPTER 10

Overview

What is a mental illness anyway? Is it any odd or eccentric behavior, or should we confine the term for more serious disturbances of behavior and thought. It sometimes seems that we lump together mental phenomena that are as disparate as the distinction between a common cold and lung cancer. Yes, both may be troublesome, and make breathing difficult, but they are very different disorders.

Not everyone who needs to be calmed or de-escalated is aggressive. However, those who display unusual or eccentric patterns of behavior are more difficult to communicate with, and when the ability of people to communicate breaks down, the risk of aggression increases.

Dispatchers shouldn't feel it incumbent upon themselves to diagnose what a caller may be suffering from, even in the most general way. This book focuses on behavior, not on illness. It isn't your job to figure out why, or even what. However, if a caller behaves in a way that makes it difficult to communicate with them, then you must have the ability to recognize certain behaviors as showing a pattern. You also need knowledge of best practice communication strategies in order to respond to a person who is displaying that pattern, whatever the cause of their behavior may be. Please note that a caller may display more than one of the behaviors described in this section. For example, they may have a rigid personality (Chapter 11), be a concrete thinker (Chapter 12), and paranoid (Chapter 17), all at the same time. Deal with whatever behavior is most detrimental to effective communication. You may have to shift from one thing to another, but as in any interaction, one or another trait will be dominant at various points in the conversation.

CHAPTER 11

Rigid Personality—
Asperger's Syndrome and Other
Similar Disorders of Relationship

Individuals with rigid personalities often have a mental disorder called Asperger's Syndrome, sometimes referred to as "high functioning autism." These people possess normal or even superior intelligence. However, they have tremendous difficulty in negotiating social interactions. They find other people to be incomprehensible, confusing, or threatening, and to make matters worse for them, they find it very difficult to figure out from facial expressions, body posture, or in the case of dispatch centers, your tone of voice, what you intend or what you are feeling. A media image that might help you understand what we are talking about is Data, the android in Star Trek, a very intelligent being who has a tremendous amount of difficulty understanding the intentions and emotions of those around him.

People with rigid personalities are often stiff and awkward socially, a little out-of-sync. Unaware of other's feelings, they can be blunt and rude. When you don't immediately understand what they are calling about, they call you stupid, not out of any malice, but from their way of thinking, their issue is something that anyone would understand. Such individuals can also be very concrete (Chapter 12) and they can get obsessively stuck on things (Chapter 14).

Such an individual can make a very challenging emergency call because they may know that there is something wrong, but they don't know exactly what it is, or how best to say it. Even though they are angry, they make pronouncements, as if reporting their emotional state, rather than expressing it. They can get wrapped up in a lot of irrelevant details. The requirements of your job demand that you have to move on to the next call as soon as possible, but with such a person, you may not, at first, even know if there is an emergency. Even when you do become aware that there is a problem, the person can get obsessively stuck on something irrelevant, and can't tell you what the emergency is.

As one child with Asperger's Syndrome said when asked what he thought the bully who beat him up was thinking, "Oh, he was thinking of Lewis and Clark." When asked with astonishment why he would be thinking of that, the child replied, in a ten minute essay, "What else could he be thinking about? Lewis and Clark took the greatest journey in history, they set out…." How do you speak with someone like this? Here are some helpful points:
- Be as concrete and literal as they are. <u>State the obvious</u>.
- <u>Explain the rules</u>. Rules are very reassuring to someone who finds human interactions chaotic or confusing. Think of the lights imbedded in the floor of an airplane that light up to show the

way in the event of an emergency. Rules serve the same function for the rigid person. *When you set such limits, DON'T SCOLD! You are giving information, not correcting or criticizing. Keep your voice calm and matter-of-fact.*

Figure 11.1 Example of Explaining the Rule

For example: "Carl, it is the rule that when you call an emergency line, you tell the call-taker the emergency first. I understand that you also are concerned about sunspot activity and its effect on the weather. But the rules require you to tell me what is dangerous right now. Carl, I understand you think that sunspots are dangerous too. Before you say another word about that, you must answer some yes or no questions:

1. "Is anyone hurt nearby?"
2. "Has anybody hurt anyone?"
3. "Is anybody planning to hurt someone?"

- Be prepared for nit-picking arguments about what might be exceptions to the rules, special conditions, etc. The person isn't trying to play games here—he/she is just trying to be as specific as possible so that they can figure out exactly how to act. At times, you will feel like you are having a discussion with a very obsessive lawyer.
- Give them <u>detailed concrete instructions</u> on what to do while waiting for emergency response. If it isn't an emergency, give them a logical alternative to follow-up on their grievance.
- Don't try to validate their feelings. Even more so, don't talk about your own feelings. As described above, other people and particularly their feelings are the most incomprehensible thing in the universe to people on the autistic spectrum.
- Stay very logical—just the facts!

Of course, lots of callers yell, lots of people nitpick, and lots of people get stuck on things. Therefore, you will probably have tried ordinary communication and de-escalation strategies first, and with most people, they are successful. They don't work with the rigid personality. If you believe you are speaking with such a person, the following example illustrates the principles of communication.

Figure 11.2 Example of a Conversation With a Rigid Personality

Pavel. "One of my neighbors has gone into my garden and picked some flowers! No one is allowed to touch any of my things! Someone is going to get socked right now!"

Call-taker. "Pavel, I want to hear about this, but you hurt my ear when you yell and I can't understand what you are saying."

Pavel. "But I want to yell. I am very angry." *(Note his lack of empathy.)*

Call-taker. "Pavel, there is a rule that one isn't allowed to yell at the emergency response dispatcher."

Pavel. "I think that is a stupid rule! I am angry and want to yell."

Call-taker. "It is still the rule. Stop shouting and we will talk."

Pavel. "I'm really mad about my roses. Someone took them. What if, while I'm talking quietly to you, I get upset again, and need to yell?"

Call-taker. "Pavel, I really want to hear about this, but you must remember the rule applies even *when* you are angry."

Pavel. "That is another stupid rule." *(You can hear him pounding the phone on an object.)*

Call-taker. "Pavel, there is another rule. It is against the rules to pound the phone while talking to the emergency dispatcher." *(Remember this officious way of talking is a last resort, after you've tried ordinary de-escalation methods, and you now believe you are dealing with a person with rigid personality).*

Pavel. "That is a REALLY stupid rule. I want to pound the phone."

Call-taker. "It is the rule. We can talk as soon as you stop pounding the phone."

Eventually, with Pavel sitting and talking quietly, you get enough details to ascertain if he is safe, or if you must send out police to make sure that he doesn't march over and assault his neighbor.

Figure 11.3 Review: Communication With Rigid Personalities

You will recognize the person with a rigid personality because they get stuck on subjects that seem rather odd in the circumstances. Furthermore, like Data in Star Trek, they seem out-of-sync with the world. They seem unconscious of their effect on others. Their emotions—if they are even displaying any—aren't those you would expect when someone calls with the complaint they have.

With such individuals you should:

- State the rules of correct behavior in a matter-of-fact way, as if simply providing information.
- Remember that validating their feelings is likely to confuse and distress them, as will talking about *your* feelings.

Once you've stabilized them, follow with a logical sequence of steps to solve their problem.

CHAPTER 12

Tell It Like It Is—
Communication With
Concrete Thinkers

When people are said to be "concrete," it means that they are very literal minded. Such people have a lot of difficulty or even a complete inability to understand metaphors, slang, or imagistic language. They may have a rigid personality (Chapter 11), be developmentally disabled, severely mentally ill, or just be a child. Latent people, described in Chapter 22, are often concrete. Ordinary communication, particularly that using "figures of speech" and imagery can be very difficult for concrete people. Below are some examples of expressions concrete people won't understand:

- "Way to go!" an expression meant as praise. The concrete individual thinks, "I'm not going anywhere." Or "Where?" Or, "Do they want me to leave now?"
- "Don't give me any attitude," an expression that means that the person shouldn't be oppositional or aggressive. The concrete individual thinks, "I'm not giving them anything," or "My attitudes are mine. How do I give them?"

Figure 12.1 Example of a Conversation With a Concrete Person

Call-taker. "Okay. So you don't have to worry anymore."

Concrete Person. "I wasn't worried. I was upset."

Call-taker. Oh, Okay, you were upset. Anyway, the police are coming, and will be there shortly. I want you to sit tight, holding the phone and talk with me."

Concrete Person. "How do I sit tight? Should I wrap myself in a blanket?"

Call-taker. *(Sigh)* "No, you don't have to wrap yourself up. I meant you should sit quietly."

Concrete Person. "You mean I shouldn't talk?"

Call-Taker. *(Aghhhhhh)* "No, you can talk! I want you to talk! It's a figure of speech!"

Figure 12.2 Last Example Correctly Done

I think you get the idea. Let us take this last example. What might be a better way to accomplish the task? Imagine this just from the call-taker's side:

- "The police are coming."
- "Tell me when they knock on the door."
- "Just sit where you are right now and keep talking to me. No, you don't have to wait by the door."
- "Oh, you can hear them knocking? Okay, I want you to do three things. But don't do anything until you have heard all three."
- That's right. Listen to all three instructions first."
- "When I say, "Go," I want you to put down the phone—that's ONE and open the door—that's TWO. Then hold your hands open where the police officers can see them."
- "Okay. Go."
- "I know, the cord is too short. Put down the phone and open the door."
- Sure, you can say goodbye to me first. Okay, goodbye."
- "Put down the phone and open the door. Then show your hands to the police. Do it now."

Figure 12.3 Review: Communication With Concrete Thinkers

You will recognize **Concrete thinkers** because they take what you say literally.

- Use clear, short sentences.
- Give directions using simple words that are easy to understand.
- Adopt a firm, calm voice.
- Show little emotion other than calm and reassurance. They will respond to your tone of voice rather than what you are saying. If you get frustrated or angry, they will usually react negatively to *your* emotions.

CHAPTER 13

Consolidating Gains

One skill that many mentally ill people develop is the art of "faking normal." People around them may do frightening things, but they don't show their fear. Other people may anger them, but they smile and pretend everything is all right. Conversations and ideas may be too complex, too fast, too metaphoric, or irrelevant to what is going on inside them, but they have learned to pick up the rhythm of the other person's speech, nod at the right moments, smile or laugh when needed, and agree with the tag lines ("right?" or "got it?") that invite such agreement. Never assume that your callers understand what you've told them to do just because they say that they do. You need to verify that they understand:

- **The least effective method to ensure that they get the information is to repeat yourself, using other words.** If they have tuned you out, or didn't understand you the first time, they may merely fake understanding.

Figure 13.1 Note on Repeating Information

This is different from the repetition of instructions we must do with the concrete (Chapter 12) or latent individual (Chapter 22). There, we are *trying to get through*. Here, we are checking to see if what we said *did* get through. Simply repeating yourself and assuming the other person understood what you've said is often a mistake.

- **Open-ended questions are more helpful than yes/no questions.** If you say, "So you will call your doctor tomorrow, won't you?" they may agree with you, hoping to please you. Instead ask, "What are you going to do tomorrow?"
- **Another method is open sentences.** Like this: "So, Joey, if I've got it right, you will talk to your dad, and tomorrow, you and your father will call the police and you will tell them about…." If they can't fill in the rest of the sentence, which is that their caregiver has been stealing, the call isn't finished yet.
- **Have the caller repeat your instructions.** Then question them about what they're supposed to do.
- **Some repeat callers keep telephoning about the same problem and don't seem to retain the answers they get.** These individuals don't learn well no matter how hard they listen. Tell them to write down the important points on a note card or sheet of paper. Have them read the notes back to you. Tell them to check their notes if they have any difficulty remembering what they are supposed to do. Discuss with them *where they will put this note, because it isn't going to help if they lose it*.

Figure 13.2 Review: How to Best Consolidate Gains

- The least effective way is to simply repeat yourself, hoping that their reply means that they did understand you, rather than merely parroting an affirmative to please you.
- Use open sentences and questions, allowing the caller to fill in the blanks.
- Have the caller repeat back your instructions.
- Have them write down the most important points on a card.

CHAPTER 14

Stuck—Coping With Repetitive Demands, Questions, and Obsessions

Some callers, particularly some of your repeat callers, will make a repetitive demand for information or otherwise seem to get "stuck" in an obsessive thought or idea. No matter how many times they get the answer, they have to ask it again. Some, who probably have Obsessive-Compulsive Disorder (OCD), are truly stuck on thoughts that obsess them. They know they are being irrational, but they still feel that they must call and speak about their obsessions, or something terrible will happen.

Others, probably psychotic, are preoccupied with their delusions, and may call, thinking, for example, that the dispatch center has access to special powers that will help them. In either event, such callers, with no malevolent intent, can tie up the emergency response system:

- Precious minutes are eaten up as you speak with them, sometimes many times a week, trying to ascertain if there is a crisis.
- Emergency response personnel are dispatched to their residence over and over, only to find that there is no emergency.

When 9-1-1 dispatchers realize that their call center has such a repeat caller, inform the supervisor. Such individuals, who eat up tremendous amounts of money and time, require a system-wide response that can be anything from aggressive outreach from a mental health agency to prosecution for false reporting and other similar charges. Please refer to Section XI: Systems Issues and Management Response for a discussion on effective response to such callers.

Other people repeat a question intending to be irritating or challenging. With these individuals, in particular, you have to clearly establish why they are on an emergency line in the first place. When a person is game-playing with questions, simply say in a neutral tone, "You already know the answer to that," or otherwise point out that they already have the information, and follow this with questions focused on what emergency they are calling about. If they don't respond with an emergency situation, the call-taker should terminate the call. If their game playing is extreme enough, these individuals, should, if possible, be prosecuted for abuse of the emergency system.

On other occasions, the caller is making a genuine plea for information, but it is "behind" the question. For example, let us say that the person, who has called on another matter, has asked, as if on a tangent, "Is it the police or Child Protective Services who go out to the house to see abused children?" You say finally, "You are really worried about children's safety, aren't you? How about you tell me why you want to know about who responds to child abuse cases. Are you worried about a child's safety?" At this point, you may get an affirmative, or you may find that you are dealing with a mentally ill person who is simply stuck on the fact that no one helped them 40 years ago when they were abused.

Figure 14 Review: Coping With Repetitive Demands, Questions, and Obsessions

You will know you are talking to an obsessive caller, because they get stuck on a subject, as if they are locked in.

- Supervisory personnel should contact the responsible law enforcement agency to discuss this problematic caller. Please refer to Section XI for more details on how the emergency response system should manage such chronic non-emergency obsessive callers. If, of course, they present as emergent, then the police will follow-up, whether or not they are obsessive.
- If a seriously mentally ill person keeps calling and asking for the same information, they may simply not be retaining it. Repeat the information and have them write the answer down. Tell them to keep it beside the phone and the next time they worry about that issue, they should look at their note before making another call.
- If the caller is trying to irritate or control you, state in a matter-of-fact voice that you have answered the question and move on. Supervisory personnel should be alerted to severe cases. Whenever possible, such manipulative individuals should face sanctions.
- *If your caller seems to have a hidden concern, state that he or she seems to be worried and find out why.*

CHAPTER 15

The Need for Reassurance

Many mentally ill people are quite anxious. Anxiety is living as if something that you fear might happen *is happening right now*. For example, you read about an earthquake in Japan and imagine what might happen to your town if an earthquake hit, and suddenly, it is as if the ground has started shaking.

Call-takers must draw a graceful line with such people. Don't coddle your caller. If you are too dismissive of their fears, you will alienate them, resulting in either anger or an increase of their anxiety. On the other hand, they may believe you if you treat them like they are too weak or frail for this world, and fail to act in a situation where they need a little courage to get moving. Make your voice matter-of-fact. If you are too delicate and solicitous, they may think that something awful is going to happen and that is why you are talking in such careful tones. At the same time, don't affect a cheerful, "You don't have to worry, you're just being silly" tone of voice. This kind of false assurance will make the caller either uneasy or irritated.

Part of true reassurance is *assurance* that you take him/her seriously, but don't indulge in what is weakest in the person. Remember, the caller who needs reassurance may be a child. You want to pass your strength through the line to him/her.

Figure 15 Review: The Need for Reassurance
When the anxious caller needs reassurance, use a confident voice that makes the person feel stronger for listening.

CHAPTER 16

Dealing With Mood Swings—
Can You Catch a Mosquito?

People with extreme mood shifts are referred to as labile. Labile individuals are very hard to communicate with because as you try to deal with one mood, they have already changed to another one. Just when you think you have achieved a moment of success, they turn on you, shifting to anger, panic, or any other extreme emotion. They can be abusive verbally, provocative, complaining, passive-aggressive, blaming, apologetic, ingratiating, and friendly all in the space of a few minutes. Such individuals may try to get control of you even when they have no control over themselves.

Coping With Mood Swings

Rather than responding to each mood the person is in, you have to become the still-point at the center (Section II). The less you are affected by their emotional storms, the more likely that they will calm down. It is the power of your calm presence that stabilizes and calms down the agitated caller who shifts from one mood to another.

Figure 16 Review: Mood Swings
People with mood swings rapidly shift emotions with no particular relationship to the situation they are in.
- Make yourself powerfully calm.
- Don't react to their mood—stay centered.
- You will be able to use many of the de-escalation tactics in Sections VIII, IX and X.

CHAPTER 17

"If There Is a Problem, That Would Be Your Fault"— Useful Tactics for Dealing With Symptoms of Paranoia and Persecution

Paranoia is a very primitive defense in which the person's motto of life could be summed up in the phrase: "If there is a problem here, that would be your fault." Paranoia isn't necessarily associated with a psychotic or delusional state, but usually with the far more common paranoid character, in which the person has a consistent attitude of blame, resentment of authority, fear of vulnerability, and an expectation of being betrayed by people they trust. *Stimulant users, notably those addicted to methamphetamine and cocaine, frequently display these behaviors.* At a core level, paranoid people are very frightened, but they cover this up with suspicion and aggression.

Such individuals are resentful of authority, because they hate to feel that someone else controls them. On the other hand, some paranoid callers may be very ingratiating, perceiving you as having a kind of power with which they want to ally themselves so that they can better defeat their enemies.

Dealing with a paranoid individual can be difficult. A sense of persecution is only part of their dilemma. Paranoid people blame others for any problems or difficulties that come up. The paranoid world is one of winners and losers. Such people try to dominate others in their lives, and they are terrified of being forced to submit.

Figure 17.1 Concerning Paranoid Delusions

If the person has paranoid delusions, then the tactics in Chapter 24 will be very useful. The principals in this chapter will help you deal specifically with the paranoid caller, whether they are delusional or not.

Paranoid people are "counter-phobic"—they are aggressive towards that which they are afraid. Imagine your caller is like a big, angry porcupine. They are actually very vulnerable—they have no quills on their stomachs, so they try to keep their backs to you all the time, hunched over and ready to strike in hair-trigger reaction.

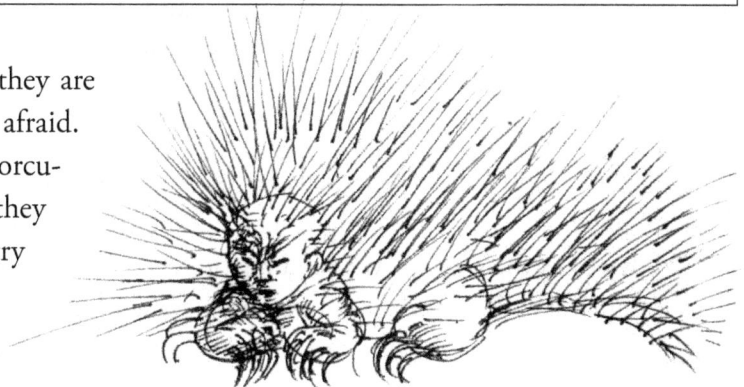

Paradoxically, paranoid people get aggressive when they begin to relax with someone. Don't be surprised, then, when the paranoid person flares up at you suddenly, just when you think you are making progress. They are torn. When they feel friendly toward you, they recoil internally. They believe that the feeling of friendship might make them vulnerable, because they assume that you are, in fact, "out to get them." They figure they might as well get it over with—so they start to use provocative ugly language, so that you show your "true colors."

Figure 17.2 Example of an Individual With a Paranoid Character Who Is Submissive and Then Turns Belligerent

An individual calls, ranting about their neighbor who has let the leaves from their maple tree fall over the property line onto their yard, yet they are, at the same time, quite humble as if using an attitude of "too-much-respect" to get you on his side. However, if you don't do what he wants, he flares up at you. Of course, this doesn't require a police response unless there is a disturbance occurring with the neighbor. Instead, refer the caller to their local government code enforcement about the leaves. However, you may need to stay on the line for threat assessment purposes in order to ascertain whether he is so heated that you need to dispatch law enforcement personnel.

Being mistaken or wrong is another form of vulnerability. Think of the words we use: "We admit our mistakes." Paranoid individuals say, "No admittance!" Because paranoid callers won't admit to wrongdoing or mistakes, they *project* negative feelings onto the other person. If, for example, you don't understand what they are saying, paranoid people believe that you are pretending because, otherwise, you'd have to admit you were wrong.

Paranoid callers live in their own world. Like detectives they search for clues and evidence to prove what they already know is true. They can have *ideas of reference*, in which they believe that other conversations, glances, or actions are directed at them, and no amount of arguing will dissuade them of these beliefs.

When paranoid people are afraid, they often attack, either verbally or physically. However, because of their aggressive or standoffish behavior, they can make other people uncomfortable or afraid. Believing you to be the same as they are, they believe you are about to attack them and not infrequently, they "hit you back" first.

Many of the communication methods we use with any delusional person are exactly the same as are used with the paranoid person. The following are some essentials specific to paranoia:
- Try to let them know what is going on. Because paranoid people are so suspicious, they will often demand to know why you are doing something. Whenever you can, answer their question. If you are going to dispatch fire or police, be as sure as you can be to let the paranoid know what to

expect, and tell him/her how to act so that they don't provoke a higher level of force on the part of the emergency responders.

- Keep a "correct" emotional distance. Don't be overly friendly. Rather, adopt a kind of a formal tone.
- Don't use feeling-based language. Remember: as far as the paranoid is concerned, whatever he feels is due to your *making him feel,* and therefore, you are taking control of him.

Figure 17.3 Review: Paranoia and Persecution

Use all the standard tactics for delusional people when speaking with a person whose delusions are paranoid. Let them know what's going on and speak to them in formal tones. Avoid feeling-based language.

SECTION IV

Recognizing the Strategies
of Manipulative and
Opportunistic Individuals

CHAPTER 18

Borderline Personality Disorder and Splitting

You most assuredly have "repeat callers." Some call many times a day. They can take up enormous resources, yet despite their often-aggravating behavior, they can be in real crises.

Many dispatch centers find themselves divided over how to deal with such individuals. You may be frustrated with other call-takers, based either on how you think they handle the calls or worse, on what you hear about those dispatchers from the callers. Anger regarding treatment of a caller is often not due to the other call-taker's incompetence. (If a co-worker's incompetence *is* the problem, then, of course, you must speak with a supervisor.) Usually, though, you should consider splitting.

Splitting is a method of defense in which an individual presents a different picture to each person with whom they interact. An individual who uses splitting is often referred to as having a borderline personality, and have usually been brought up in a dangerous, chaotic environment. He/she learned, quite early, to use a "divide and confuse" strategy, presenting a different "face" to fit whatever they think each person they interact with wants. In other cases, they use behaviors that they think will help them control the other people they are dealing with.

Unfortunately, this strategy, which is the best a frightened child can create, is ineffective for functioning in normal society. Such a person never learns how to relate to others—they know merely how to react to them. And not surprisingly, they are frequently "off base:"

- They misinterpret the intentions of others.
- They often have a poor grasp on their effect on other people, as well as how to actually speak to others.
- They don't know how to get what they truly desire. This is the kind of person who, expecting a refusal, won't ask politely for something. Instead, they might try to get it through a guilt trip, a demand, blame, or trickery. They may resent the person who hasn't given them what they want, even though they never asked for it directly.

Such callers go everywhere for help, often presenting with serious problems. They speak to various dispatchers, crisis line personnel, hospitals, mental health professionals, etc. Each of the responders may think that they've got the best idea on how to deal with the person, and this can result in backbiting or out-and-out arguments between individuals and/or agencies.

How to Deal With Splitting

From a call-taker's perspective, <u>the task is to stay on task</u>. If the caller isn't calling about an emergency, they need to get off the line. Don't get distracted by their complaints about other call-takers or other people involved in their situation. If there is an emergency, stay focused on *that* and don't respond to their negative blaming, their manipulative statements, and/or complaints.

Particularly when the person is a repeat caller, their behaviors demand a systems response, both among staff in your call center, and sometimes encompassing the larger system: law enforcement, mental health providers, emergency medical responses, etc. This will be discussed in Section XI.

Figure 18 Review: Dealing With Splitting
- Stay focused on whether or not there is an emergent issue.
- Don't be reactive to the manipulative complaints and/or side issues.
- If they are a frequent caller, this requires a system-wide response or they will drain considerable time, resources, and money.

CHAPTER 19

Bad Intentions—
Recognizing the Strategies
of Manipulative Callers

Some people don't mean us well. They view us as opportunities to gain something they want or as animated toys to be played with. Others live for hate and destruction, but delight most in duping people so that they don't even know how "dirty they were done." Here are a number of manipulative verbal gambits. If they come up in a call, you are at least warned that there is a game going on.[2]

- **Lies of omission.** They will tell you reassuring aspects of a situation, but not include their intention to harm.

Figure 19.1 Example: Lie of Omission

You are speaking to someone with a criminal history. You are getting the information regarding safety for the EMT if they were to go to the house. He, anticipating your concern, says: "My roommate's here. She's cool. I guess you are a little uncomfortable sending someone to my apartment based on my history. Don't worry. I'm not like the other people in this situation."

Notice that neither of the statements establishes, in the slightest, that he doesn't mean to assault the EMT when he/she arrives.

- **Reassuring promise.** One sign of coercion is a reassuring promise when none was asked for.

Figure 19.2 Example of Reassuring Promise

"Yeah, I know my kid is crying. My other daughter's taking care of him. There's nothing wrong with her. You know, I'm thinking, given all the things that are blown up on TV that you might be concerned about the question of abuse. I'm a great father. That's not why I'm calling."

- **Too much information.** One way to manage the perceptions of others is to talk too much, too elaborately. Instead of information, you get a story.

Figure 19.3 Examples: Too Much Information

#1

"Do I have the guns locked away? Of course I do. I used to be a city councilman, and we had a gun ordinance, we were concerned about child safety, and a lot of citizens didn't care for law enforcement, you know, all that left wing disrespect we have these days. People today just don't love our country."

In this case, the manipulator does have the guns locked away, but he will unlock them before the first responders arrive. He attempts to portray himself as a trustworthy guy, so that the dispatcher won't look for and acquire information that would put the first responders in a state of heightened alert.

#2

"Ok, Ok, sorry for all the questions and arguments. Ok. I do have a gun. I just have this first amendment thing going on. It's a Glock. Tell you what, police are on the way, I don't want them to worry. It'll be on the sidewalk, clip out and unloaded. They don't have to worry about me."

Good news, right? But if he played things right, you won't ask if he has any other weapons, or in the relief that he "gave" it up, you will assume he is actually working with you, as opposed to setting your people up.

- Use of Personal Information. Manipulative people try to acquire information that you won't want revealed. In other cases, they try to use the personal information in an attempt to make you think you have something in common with them.

Figure 19.4 Example: Use of Personal Information

"Whoa, wait a minute. That accent! You are from Alabama, aren't you? I'm from Birmingham. I'm so glad to be talking to someone from home. A bad situation like this—it's a relief, let me tell you that."

- **Quid-pro-quo.** If people do us a favor, we humans feel like we owe them. By making it very hard to get information or work with them deliberately, and then offering information that was long awaited, they may be trying to get you to let down your guard, because they "came around."
- **Blaming.** If manipulators don't get what they want, they may complain bitterly how they trusted the dispatcher, and this is what happens.

Figure 19.5 Example: Blaming

"Honestly, when I called here, I didn't expect much anyway. Men have always treated me badly. But I thought that, given you were a 9-1-1 dispatcher, I could trust you. I should have known better"

- Attacks best and/or weak points. The manipulator will attack you not only through your weak points, but also your best points. The manipulator scans his/her victim looking for leverage, and they are equally skilled at using your weak points *and* your strong points against you.

Figure 19.6 Example: Attack of Weak and Best Points

- If you are religious, you very likely have a faith in the redemption of people. A caller showing contrition, even in a non-religious context, may lead you to let down your guard.
- Let us say that one of your proudest attributes is your willingness to help the underdog. The manipulator will "become" a victim of oppression, and then, when there should be a suspicion that he/she is out of line, you might mentally defend the person and not pick up the warning signs that they are dangerous.

- **Grooming behavior.** The manipulative person may set up a situation where he/she creates in you a little anxiety and then relieves it *while making a request you would have granted anyway.*

Figure 19.7 Example: Grooming Behavior

You are worried that the caller might harm her child. She talks about her anger, and your anxiety mounts. Then in a warm tone, she tells you how much she loves her baby and then asks your advice as to whether you think the local mental health center helps mothers like her. In your sense of relief, you don't realize that you never did get all the information necessary to determine if the baby is, in fact, safe.

- **Conscious splitting.** (See Chapter 18 regarding *unconscious* splitting) Manipulators *deliberately* split by spreading rumors or stories about other staff or callers.

Figure 19.8 Example: Conscious Splitting

"Can I ask a question? I've been told I could trust the dispatchers here. Umm—I don't know exactly *how to say* this, but I was talking to another dispatcher—that guy with the Irish accent and he said that one thing he hates about the job is working with a lot of fat women. I mean, I have issues with my weight, and he said he couldn't stand women who won't take care of themselves. I don't know if I feel safe calling a place where you have a guy like that working there."

- **Victim role.** Manipulators will often use a victim role, even a real history, as leverage, trying to elicit "privileged guilt."

Figure 19.9 Example: Victim Role

- "You've never lived our kind of life"
- "I wish I had the kind of chances you had. I probably wouldn't be here today."

- **Flirtation.** If you don't address flirtation and come-ons right away it is viewed as implicit acceptance. You are now open to blackmail, and/or at minimum, an escalation of such approaches. Another thing some manipulators will do is let others know about your "acceptance" of the flirtation.

Figure 19.10 Example: Flirtation

You work in a small call center, with only three staff, two women and one man—a caller, whose mother has had several cardiac events, flirts with one of the female dispatchers. When she puts him in his place, he adopts a hurt tone, and says, "I don't get it. I called last week, my mom was having trouble then too, and after it was solved, the other lady dispatcher didn't act like you. All I did was compliment your voice—it's prettier than hers actually, and she didn't make a big deal about it. What's the matter with women today? Some of you just can't take a compliment. At least that other dispatcher acts like a lady."

- **Manipulative language.** Manipulative language can include the following (in addition to that already enumerated above):
  a. Denial of personal responsibility. "I got caught up in something." Or "Nobody told me."
  b. Minimizing. "I made a mistake."
  c. "You know what I mean." (Or you would, if you were cool.)
  d. "Honestly" or "I'll tell you the truth" or "I wouldn't lie to you."
  e. You are like all the rest. "I should have known you wouldn't understand."

SECTION V

Communication With People Suffering
From Severe Mental Illness
or Other Conditions That
Cause Severe Disability

CHAPTER 20

Overview

This section offers detailed descriptions of the most significant behaviors that mentally ill callers may display, regardless of diagnosis. Along with each description will be suggestions for the best way to communicate with such callers. Please note, however, that a lot of the strategies in various sections overlap. Some are generally applicable, while others are specific to only one type of behavior/symptom. Just because you might be reading about paranoia, for example, doesn't mean that such a person isn't also disorganized, delusional, or manic. What you are trying to develop is a range of communication tactics that cover as many situations as possible.

Mental illness, in this vein, doesn't only refer to such disorders as schizophrenia, bipolar disorder or depression. For example, intoxication can be considered a time limited, substance induced mental disorder. Beyond any medical condition, people, otherwise normal, can display acute, "out of character" behaviors, due to problems or stressors in their lives. Thus, for the sake of this discussion, substance abuse, distinct neurological disorders, as well as atypical episodes brought on by stress or other factors, all function as mental illness. The cause may be relevant if making appropriate referrals for treatment; the call-taker, however, should most emphatically focus on the behaviors, whatever the cause.

The Undamaged Self

You are walking outside on an icy winter day. You slip suddenly and spin toward the pavement. You thrust out an arm that breaks your fall. It also breaks your right wrist. Your life, for a few weeks or months, is different. Even the simplest tasks are difficult and may require assistance. Still, even though you are inconvenienced, and the injury probably changes your mood quite a bit, you are still "you," the same person as before your injury. In due time, your injuries will heal, the accident forgotten, as you continue through life. Such isn't the case with mental illness.

Severe mental illness can cause mental and emotional disturbances far more profound than the temporary inconveniences brought on by physical injury. One's ability to think is distorted, and with delusions, reality is skewed. Perceptions may be bizarre, even hallucinatory. Emotions swing from high to low, or shift into realms at odds with one's immediate circumstances. Mental illness is an assault on one's worldview, but **there is still a person behind the symptoms.** Mentally ill callers aren't simply bundles of raw emotions or distorted cognitions. There exists an essential part of each of them untouched by their mental illness. We can choose to speak to the illness, or speak to the *person* who is ill. That core part of his/her psyche is the person we are trying to reach, not only for human reasons, but also tactical reasons as well.[3]

CHAPTER 21

Struggling in a Fog—
Dealing With Confusion
and Disorganization

Understanding Disorganization

Disorganization is a very general term for an inability to adequately organize thinking, perceptions, and/or feelings so that a person can function stably. Disorganized people often also show behaviors such as latency (Chapter 22) and/or concrete thinking (Chapter 12).

- Such people may be severely *autistic* (as opposed to high functioning autistic people, described in Chapter 11). The severely autistic are overwhelmed by the emotional communications of people, as well as the enhanced sensory impressions that they receive.
- Individuals with Alzheimer's Disorder or other forms of dementia often become disorganized, as do those with head injuries and a variety of other neurological disorders.
- Developmentally delayed individuals, often referred to as "mentally retarded," often lack the maturity to manage complex or frustrating situations. In addition, due to their cognitive limitations, they aren't skilled at problem-solving.
- Acutely intoxicated individuals—drunk or stoned—are usually disorganized.
- *Seriously* mentally ill people also become disorganized. Delusional people can be quite focused, if only on their delusions. When one becomes disorganized, however, even one's delusions break down into chaos, manifesting as incoherent speech.

Figure 21.1 Review: Typical Behaviors of Disorganized People
You will know you are dealing with a disorganized person because:
- They are incoherent, or otherwise impossible to communicate with.
- They seem to shift from one emotion to another with no logical reason.
- It is very hard, if not impossible to hold their attention.

Small Bits at a Time

When you speak with callers who are disorganized, long involved sentences or intense emotional communication plunge them into chaos. Make sure that you are very specific in what you tell them to do. Instructions should also be simple. There is no point in being irritable with such a person. It simply makes it even harder for them, because they usually don't know why you are upset and this becomes an added disorganizing factor.

Repeat Yourself

When we aren't understood, our usual impulse is to elaborate: we use different words, or we intensify our emotional tone. With disorganized people, it is often better to just repeat the same statement or question word-for-word. You may need to do this four, five times or more. The aim isn't to browbeat them. Don't shout to get through to them. Repetition is a touchstone of stability. It allows your caller to focus because it becomes their one consistent point of reference. Try to get them to repeat your instructions as well. They can sometimes begin to grasp what you are saying when they say it themselves.

Acceptance of Magical Thinking

Magical thinking is a term that overlaps with delusions (Chapter 24). Magical thinking is common among small children, senile and demented adults, and individuals who are delayed developmentally.

Unlike delusions however, magical thinking isn't "locked in." Delusional people tend to be fixated: in other words, it is very hard to get them to change the subject. Magical thinking, on the other hand, is "childlike"—you can often deflect the person to another topic, just as you can with a child who is "telling stories." People displaying magical thinking have a different "energy" than someone who is delusional. They come off as naïve or boastful—the delusional person is as fixed as a heat-seeking missile.

Magical thinking is sometimes caused by confusion. One caller may believe that you are his grandmother. You sound the same—kind and warm—and he has been thinking of his grandmother all day, so it is no surprise to him that he is talking to her.

Magical thinking can also be a kind of fable making—the kinds of stories very young people tell—either young in age or young in mind. Often they fantasize that they are some kind of hero.

Figure 21.2 Example: Magical Thinking

Luke, who is delayed developmentally, tells long, convoluted stories that he is a secret agent for the CIA, and once was a hit-man, but no one has to worry anymore because he's retired. "You know the <u>Bourne Identity</u>? That movie was about me. People don't believe me because I'm overweight, but when you have training, that's just a form of camouflage. Nobody would suspect me. Actually, most of my training is ninja kind of stuff. I can climb walls and things. They sometimes used to have me just carry a sword, because no one would expect a secret agent to have a sword."

Once you realize that such a caller is subject to magical thinking, and they are talking about non-emergent fantasies, say, with a little tiredness in your voice, "Let's not talk about that anymore. Luke, you have to tell me what you are calling about right now. What is the emergency?"

The Use of the Dramatic Voice

Sometimes, you can use a dramatic voice with a child or a person who seems to be disorganized or has some kind of developmental disability. In this case, you DO make your voice a little louder, and you use a lot of energy to grab their attention. Think of how you are when you meet a child, perhaps one who is a little shy. He/she shows you a favorite toy, and you respond, "Wow, you REALLY like that car, don't you!"

Figure 21.3 Example: Use of Dramatic Voice

You have a caller, on a cell phone. You don't know her location. You realize that she has called from a group home for developmentally disabled adults. She is hysterically upset, because one of the other residents hit their caregiver, the only responsible adult, in the head. The victim is unconscious. Other residents are milling around, while the aggressive man is in the kitchen, trashing things. Your caller is wailing and crying, and no matter how strong and focused you make your voice, she continues to sob, and in answer to your questions, sobs, "I don't know! I don't know!" So you change your voice. Imagine you are speaking in a "wow! Aren't you a big girl" tone.

"Joanie, I am SO PROUD of you that you called. You are so BRAVE. And I BET you are BRAVE ENOUGH to do something else. Yes, you ARE. I know you are. Find a piece of mail and read the address to me." *(Small delay)* "What? There is no mail. And Joey says he will hit you next? Okay, Listen Joanie, you are so SMART. I know you are BRAVE enough to do something else! Walk out of the front door. Yes, I know, you aren't supposed to leave without Mrs. Oldham, but she can't go with you. So I'm the one you listen to. Yes! Okay, ready? Out the door—let's go out the door. Take the phone with you! Good girl! Can you tell me numbers? Yeah? What's the number on the house? 437? What a smart young lady! Okay can you see the end of the street? You can? Is there a street sign? Uh-huh. Great. Now here's where we get even braver. Let's go to the street sign...."

Figure 21.4 Review: Dealing With an Individual With Symptoms of Disorganization

You will know you are dealing with a disorganized person because they are:

- Nearly incoherent, or otherwise impossible to communicate with.
- They seem to shift from one emotion to another with no logical reason.
- It is very hard, if not impossible to hold their attention.

You will:

- Divide tasks into small bits.
- Give simple, specific instructions.
- Be realistic about what your caller can and can't do.
- Repeat your instructions rather than elaborate on them. Don't change your vocal tone.
- Don't argue with magical thinking: redirect them to discussing what, if anything is emergent.
- Use a dramatic voice with children and with those who seem to be childlike

CHAPTER 22

Dropping Stones in a Well—
Latency

Latency is a behavior where people respond to communication in an inordinately slow manner. You might ask a question and they stare vacantly, or they talk quietly to themselves as they puzzle out what you might be saying. Others "respond" with long periods of silence after you speak to them or ask a question.

Many such people may be hearing hallucinatory voices, or be overwhelmed by stimuli from outside—the glitter of light on the varnish of a piano and the white keys that look like teeth, for example, or the static on the phone line—and your words seem very far away. Others may be cognitively impaired with Alzheimer's Disorder, dementia, or intellectual/developmental disabilities and they simply don't understand what you are saying, or even more severe, don't even realize that they should reply to what you say.

Imagine your words like a stone dropping into a well. You expect to hear it hit bottom. When you don't hear a splash, you drop another stone into the well, and yet another. Now imagine the latent individual's mind also like a well, but very old, with bricks sticking out, and tree roots a-tangle halfway down. The first stone hits the roots, bounces off a brick and then another and another but it gradually does get to the bottom. When you throw one stone after another, your listeners now have three pebbles bouncing around, and they get more and more confused.

Figure 22.1 Recognizing Latency
You will recognize latency when the person you are speaking with not only delays his/her answers an amazingly long time, but when they do speak, their communication is often somewhat odd and disjointed, or not really a responds to the question you asked.

Coping With Latency
When communicating with an individual with latency do the following:
- **Keep your sentences short, and simple.** Ask basic questions, and give clear instructions. Minimize all the qualifiers ("you might" "maybe" "kind of," etc.) that you ordinarily put in your sentences.
- **Keep your voice on an even level.** Try to minimize your changeable vocal tones. I don't mean you should talk like a robot, but an overly emotional vocal tone—*any emotion*—will prove to be

very distracting to the latent individual. They will respond to your changed tone of voice rather than to what you are saying, and become MORE latent rather than less.

- **Repeat.** Latent people usually **don't** need you to explain things in more detail. They simply didn't get it the first time. Say the same thing again, but don't use a frustrated tone, or speak as if you are going through the motions. You must put the same interest and focus in each repetition. Remembering the image of dropping the pebbles in the well: rather than a new stone, you add weight to the one already there. Repetition gives it, metaphorically, "double mass." Now it can get through the roots and bricks and hit bottom—the place of understanding.
- <u>**Try to get the caller to repeat your instructions back to you**</u>.

Figure 22.2 Review: Latency

You will recognize latency when the person you are speaking with not only delays his/her answers an amazingly long time, but when they do speak, their communication can be somewhat odd, disjointed or not really responding to the question you asked. Deal with latency by:

- Keep your sentences short.
- Repeat the instructions using the same words and the same tone of voice.
- Whenever possible, try to get the caller repeat back your instructions.

CHAPTER 23

Withdrawal From
Intoxicating Substances

This is almost always a medical emergency. If there are other people in the house, get them on the line and give them instructions on:

- What to do to keep themselves safe, depending on the behavior of the withdrawing person.
- Any instructions you can give on how best to keep the withdrawing person safe, if this doesn't compromise their own safety.

If the withdrawing person is alone, your responsibility is to keep them calm until emergency medical personnel and/or police arrive. People in withdrawal are often in pain or feeling quite ill. The signs of withdrawal can include:

- Unstable coordination. (You might hear them lurching around or dropping the phone.) You must try to get them to sit or lie down for their safety.
- Restlessness and agitation. Try to reduce any stimulating input. Tell them to turn off their music, if it is loud, or go to a more quiet area of the house.
- Unpredictable and sudden actions. Get them focused on your voice.
- Slurred speech or sometimes talking in complete gibberish. Speak to them in a strong, firm voice and make an extra effort to understand what they are saying. Provide short explanations.
- Most importantly, they are often very argumentative and demanding. There is no specific withdrawal rage. Try to redirect them or de-escalate depending on the mode of anger or rage they exhibit. (See the later sections of this book on de-escalation of aggression.)

CHAPTER 24

Communication With Psychotic Callers— Understanding Delusions and Hallucinations

What is a delusion?

A *delusion* is a belief that doesn't fit reality—sort of. Actually, it's a lot more than that. There are lots of people who have strange beliefs: unconventional religious ideas, dietary and health habits that range from fruit and water to high protein and fat, or beliefs in aliens, crop circles, and telepathy. It's possible that some of those are *your* beliefs. They are eccentric to me but not to you. Unique ideas and beliefs aren't, however, delusional.

A delusional belief doesn't even have to be unusual. I might state that the FBI is following me. The FBI *does* follow people. I may believe that I am getting special wisdom every time I read the Bible. That puts me in a group with hundreds of millions of people. The hallmark of a delusional belief is its "locked-in" quality. It has the same relation to an ordinary belief as a cult has to a religion. People leave churches all the time and find new ones, or go to no church whatsoever. A cult, however, is far more difficult to leave. People are ground down in cults so that they no longer can question beliefs. They are locked into cult doctrine. Delusions are like cults with one member.

When people become delusional, it is as if they have had a revelation. All the confusing thoughts they have had, all the worries, prayers, fantasies, or ideas suddenly coalesce into **BELIEF**. Such beliefs are unshakable, unarguable, and unalterable by conflicting evidence.

Types of Delusions

Grandiose delusions. People believe that they have been appointed for a special mission, that they have special powers, or are special, remarkable people.

Religious delusions. Sometimes linked with grandiose delusions, people become preoccupied with religion, focusing all their attention on their beliefs, which may be self-made or associated with mainstream doctrines.

Jealous delusions. People believe, irrationally and against all evidence, that their partners are unfaithful to them. This is beyond even severe jealousy, where the individual reacts with rage or despair out of either suspicion or knowledge that the object of their affections might be interested in someone else. A jealous delusion, however, is a locked-in, false belief that betrayal is occurring, <u>contrary</u> to any evidence that it isn't.

<u>Delusional stalking.</u> People believe that another person is in love with them, is married to them, or has been, somehow, designated as theirs, whether they know it or not.

<u>Persecutory (paranoid) delusions.</u> People believe that they have enemies: people, or powers that have hostile intentions toward them, or may be committing evil actions. The paranoid is a "grandiose victim." Such individuals often have "ideas of reference." They believe that others are sending energy towards them, thinking about them, talking about them, or looking at them.

<u>What are hallucinations?</u>

A **hallucination** is a disturbance in perception. One perceives things in ways that don't conform to reality. One can experience hallucinations with any one of the senses. Hallucinations are often, but not always, accompanied by delusions. It is possible that a person can hallucinate and be aware that their mind is playing tricks on them; for example, hearing voices when jet-lagged for too many days. However, most people who are psychotic, are both delusional *and* have hallucinations—having false perceptions and false beliefs.

Types of Hallucinations

<u>Auditory hallucinations.</u> There are two levels of hallucinations perceived through hearing. The first level is **auditory distortion**. What is said is misheard. This very frequently is part of persecutory delusions. For example, a paranoid person is in the middle of a restaurant, and hears someone say, "Do you want to get the chicken or the ribs?" What they hear is, "Do you want to get that chicken in the ribs?" The second level is true **auditory hallucinations**. This isn't imagination—it is an experience. Close your eyes *when someone speaks* to you. Do you still hear their voice? When people have an auditory hallucination, it is as clear and real as that. That is why you can't simply say, "The voice isn't real." That makes as much sense to them as someone telling you that your foot isn't real.

<u>Visual hallucinations.</u> Here, too, are two levels. People can experience **visual distortions;** *visual perceptions* appearing to move, melt, emerge towards you, or even speak. Think of a Salvador Dali painting in which the objects melt and flow. Imagine tiny eyes appearing in the granite surface of your countertop, or little fingers emerging from the cracks in the walls.

The second level is true **visual hallucinations**. Objects appear that no one else can see. They can be inanimate or alive. Perhaps there are flowers blooming from the floor, or an angel hovering overhead—in either case, only the hallucinating person can see them.

Olfactory hallucinations. This refers to smells. This is sometimes a sign of brain injury, as the part of the brain that detects smells is at the front of the head, a frequent target of blows. Sometimes people get focused on their own body smells, and believe, for example, that they are rotting away. Other times, people believe they can smell poison gas seeping through the walls. Anytime you have a caller who complains of what sound like olfactory hallucinations, consider this a possible medical emergency related to head injury or other neurological damage. Alert police or EMT that the caller is experiencing olfactory hallucinations and that according to training you have received, this may be related to a possible head injury. Aside from the medical issue, head injured people are high assault risks.

Tactile hallucinations. These are sensations within the body. Bugs crawling in the limbs are frequently a side effect of drugs such as methamphetamine or cocaine. It can also be a side effect of the person's psychiatric medication. Other people have complained of experiencing sexual invasion or of snakes crawling into their bodies.

The Torment of Hallucinations
Hallucinations torment their victims in a variety of ways:
- For unknown reasons, hallucinated voices are almost always cruel. People can be ordered to do awful or degrading things, or they may simply hear awful sounds and ugly demeaning words. Visual hallucinations can be as haunting as ghosts. Olfactory hallucinations are often foul odors, and tactile hallucinations are almost always very unpleasant sensations.
- People try to tell others what they perceive, but their experience is denied over and over again. They can be teased or laughed at.
- Many people find that their worldview is called into question every day. They don't know what is real and what isn't. Imagine reaching to pick up your tea and not knowing if the liquid will disappear from the cup or if the cup handle will suddenly twine around your finger like a little snake. Imagine this is true of every object in your life.

General Strategies for Communicating With People With Delusions and Hallucinations
There are specific requirements on how to communicate with people who have delusions of being persecuted (Chapter 17). Delusion stalkers, who will be discussed below, also require specific interventions. First, however, here are some general strategies for communicating with people who have either delusions or hallucinations.

It can be very draining to talk with a delusional person. Like cultists trying to convert you to their group, they may try to convince you that what they believe is real. They may insist that you should believe what they do, or even more problematic, insist that you *do* believe the same, but simply won't admit it. You try to argue with them, and they may get even more intent on debating past your resistance or furious that you deny what is, to them, absolutely true.

There is often no good reason to continue the discussion. Delusions aren't like some sort of backed-up fluid that you vent and drain away. The more the person talks about their delusions, the more agitated they become. Discussion and argument seem to cement the delusions even further—the more one talks about it, the more one believes it to be true.

Figure 24.1 Rule #1: Disengage

There are many occasions when nothing at all can be accomplished by talking about delusions or hallucinations. There is no emergency, and no need for investigation or information gathering. In such cases, disengage.

Threat Assessment: When should you talk about the delusions?

Let us imagine that your caller is sure that she is the Archangel Michael. If you recall this biblical story, Michael casts Satan out of Heaven. Michael is power incarnate, the righteous sword of the Lord God. Imagine that your caller sometimes believes she perceives Satan's work in the behavior of people around her. She once tried to acquire a sword at an antique shop to slay demons. Had she not praised the dealer of the sword for his help in accomplishing God's work in eliminating Satan, the police won't have been called, and the family down the street whom she believed to be the minions of Satan could have been maimed or killed.

When such a delusional person calls 9-1-1, and begins to talk about God, angels, Satan, or anything else that touches on her delusions, ask questions about what he/she is preoccupied with.
- "Joanie, are you telling me that you think you have seen Satan? Where?
- "Why do you think that what you saw is Satan's work?"
- "Do you think you should do anything about this?"
- "What do you think you should do?"

If Joanie's answers are bland and not aggressive, then you can, at the appropriate time, change the subject. As soon as you are sure that she presents no danger, you can terminate the call expeditiously. Whenever possible, ask it they are alone. If there is someone else with them, try to get them to put that person on the phone to verify what is happening.

If, however, her answers might be potentially dangerous, then action would be required. For example, if she were to say, "Don't call me Joanie!—I'm Michael, the Lord's most beloved angel. Satan will have no place on this earth when I take my righteous sword in my strong right arm!" Then you must dispatch police NOW. Dangerous answers are an alarm call to get help, not only for her, but also for her potential victims. She may have to have her medications adjusted, or need a stay in the hospital.

> ## Figure 24.2 Rule #2 Talk About the Delusions for Threat Assessment
> Talk about the delusions as a means of threat assessment. Don't be afraid to ask direct questions concerning the caller's particular intention to hurt himself/herself or others. If the caller doesn't bring it up perhaps he/she is withdrawn or reluctant. You bring the subject up yourself, to ascertain if there is an immediate or potential risk of harm.

Islands of Sanity: When should you change the subject?

Imagine being dropped overboard into the ocean. It is cold and rough among the waves, and there are all kinds of sea-life that demands your attention—everything from sharks to jellyfish. Like the delusional world, there seems to be no way out. It is so overwhelming that one can't take one's mind off it.

Even in the ocean, however, there are small patches of land—islands. If you can only get to one of them, you can put your feet down on solid ground. For delusional people, too, there are "islands of sanity," areas of their lives where they aren't delusional. They may be convinced, for example, that someone is poisoning their food, and only canned goods are safe to eat and drink, or that someone is beaming messages directly into their brain. Let us imagine, however, that you begin talking about football with such a delusional man, and as you and he begin going over how the Pittsburgh Steelers demolished yet another opponent, he, without even realizing it, takes his mind off his delusions, enabling him to experience a moment of respite.

> ## Figure 24.3 Rule #3 Move Toward the Islands of Sanity
> As the delusional person speaks, pay attention to areas of thought and subjects where he/she isn't delusional. Once you have completed your threat assessment, in regards to their delusions or hallucinations, try to change the subject. Talking about delusions can often make the situation worse. Talking about the "islands of sanity" helps the person to stabilize, making it easier for you to sort out if today's call is, in fact, emergent. This can also be useful to keep the caller stable, while emergency personnel are in transit. This is also useful with repeat callers, who usually call in an agitated state. Once you ascertain that they aren't in an emergent situation, shift to the "island of sanity," so that they calm down, allowing you to terminate the call.

Don't Agree: At Least Most of the Time

It might seem to be easiest to take the line of least resistance—simply agree with the delusions, or pretend that you, too, perceive the hallucinations rather than get caught in arguments. However, there are a number of problems in doing so:

- When you agree with delusions and/or hallucinations, you will entrench them deeper into the individual's pathological belief system. Given that most delusional ideas, at minimum, make life harder for the person, and some are truly dangerous, it's hard to view this as a good idea.

Figure 24.4 Example: Danger of Agreeing With a Delusion and /or Hallucination

Charles began to believe that his cousin Giorgio and he were part of the same rock band. One day, he was convinced that Giorgio had stolen a song that they had co-written and sold it to a major record label. He heard it on the radio every day, but he hadn't been paid for it. He began to call the emergency dispatch center, demanding that police arrest Giorgio. If Charles believes that the dispatcher agrees with him, yet isn't calling the police to arrest Giorgio, it makes the possibility of an assault even more likely.

- Sometimes when you agree with delusions or hallucinations, you can be incorporated into the delusional system. Sometimes this can be benign, but wearying, and they begin to call 9-1-1 incessantly.
- Just because someone is mentally ill doesn't mean they are gullible, and sooner or later, they will realize that you are pretending to believe them. This can enrage the delusional person, and there is no way of predicting who will become their target.

Figure 24.5 Example: Agreement Gone Wrong

The dispatcher began agreeing with the Jeremiah's delusions because nothing else seemed to work. He hoped that Jeremiah would be satisfied and not call so often. Jeremiah was fixated about the synagogue down the street, believing that neo-Nazis would bomb it. The Operator would say, "Yep, those Nazis are dangerous. I hope you are keeping an eye out for them." However, Jeremiah realized that he was being brushed off—that the dispatcher was patronizing him. He was furious and decided that the best way to show the dispatcher, and by extension, the police how upset he'd become was to march to the call center bearing a shotgun to confront the dispatcher.

Figure 24.6 Experience: An Account of Successfully Joining Another's Delusional System

I recall a man who thought he was still in Vietnam. He showed up at a random house in his military fatigues, his face painted with black stripes and with his AK-47 took a family hostage. I could hear the family screaming for help and crying in the background. The man spoke as if I were his command officer and that he had "captured" the enemy. I played the part of his commanding officer and gave him orders until police had their perimeter set-up. I then had him put his weapon down, and he came out with his hands in the air. He was taken into custody with no physical injuries to anyone.

CAUTION: Stories like this can really encourage you to try this strategy. It should be the rarest of interventions, to be used only in a life-threatening situation. There are so many ways it can backfire, including the delusional person now no longer trusting emergency personnel to tell him the truth. The next time and there very likely will be a next time, there will be no talking with him.

Figure 24.7 Rule #4: Don't Agree With Delusions

In almost all circumstances, don't agree with the person's delusions. This will entrench the delusions further; get the caller dangerously fixated on the 9-1-1 dispatcher; or will enrage the caller when they perceive they are being conned.

Don't Disagree: At Least Most of the Time

Common sense seems to demand that you speak for what is real. When people see something that isn't there, shouldn't you tell them so? If they have an irrational belief, why not argue them out of it, or at least, diplomatically point out where they are wrong. This, too, can engender all sorts of problems.

You are arguing *reality* with someone. Look around your room. What color are your walls? If I go to your home and tell you they are red when they are pale green, you won't believe me, no matter how many times I repeat myself, no matter how much intensity I direct at you, will you? If you are having a conversation with your daughter, will you believe me if I tell you that she is an iguana? The fundamental problem with arguing with delusional or hallucinating people is that you are telling them that their senses and their brains are lying to them. Even though you are right, they won't believe you.

Figure 24.8 Rule #5: Don't Disagree With Delusions

In almost all circumstances, don't disagree with the person's delusions. This will set you at odds with the caller, or enrage them. Exceptions are psychotic stalkers and pathologically jealous individuals, both of whom should receive an adamant contradiction from the call-taker, or a delusional person who, unusually, pleads for a reality check.

Exceptions to the "Don't Disagree" Rule

Stalking delusions are particularly dangerous because they involve another person as focus of the delusions. "Conditional demurrals" may be taken as agreement. For this reason, the stalker should NOT hear from you, "Look, sometimes these things are confusing. I know you think she loves you, but she has a different point of view." The stalker has a selfish, entitled sense of his/her own right to approach, or harass the victim. This is a crime. The victim needs to be protected. Similarly, you shouldn't validate, in any way, a caller who is expressing pathological jealous delusions.

Sometimes delusional people ask or even plead with you for disagreement because they don't want to believe what their delusions seem to tell them. At other times, a hallucinating person can make a tenuous distinction between real perceptions and hallucinations and will ask you if you think something hallucinated **is** real. In these cases, *when you have been invited*, it is acceptable to state that not only do you not perceive or believe the hallucination or delusion, but you <u>also</u> don't think it is real.

Differentiation: The Golden Mean (If you can't agree or disagree, what *can* you do?)

There is no more lonely experience than to be psychotic. Your delusional beliefs can so preoccupy you that there is almost no moment that they aren't part of your thoughts, or just when you think you are at peace, an ugly voice suddenly rises out inside your head and accuses you of something obscene. Much of this is impossible to talk about. People simply disbelieve you, or minimize what troubles or preoccupies you, telling you to stop imagining things. Even the people you love become tainted by the psychotic experience.

When your caller voices a delusion or talks about a hallucination, the surest way to make that vital distinction between your world and theirs is to *differentiate*. The goal here is to not argue about the mentally ill person's perception of reality. You validate that they perceive what they perceive—but you also assert that you don't perceive the same. Thereby, you have a better chance of actually ascertaining what the emergency is, because you are less likely to get in an argument about reality.

Figure 24.9 Examples: Differentiation

- "Hans, I only hear two voices on the phone—yours and mine. I don't hear a woman's voice at all. What do *you* hear her say?"
- "Will, I know you believe that the Democrats and Republicans are secretly managed by Al Qaeda. I'm not arguing with you. I simply don't know anything about this. What is the emergency you are calling about?"

Figure 24.10 Rule #6: Differentiation

Give the person the "right" to their own perceptions and beliefs. You inform them that *you* don't perceive what they do, but you aren't arguing with them about their perceptions

Steam-valve: When the Pressure Is Too Great

Some people, either psychotic or manic, are so full of things to say, think, or feel that they seem like they are going to explode from the pressure. Their speech can become pressured as well. Words cascade out of them in floods of thought and flights of ideas. Sometimes they make sense, but they dominate the "air time," and neither allows you to speak or to change the subject to something that must be attended to. Other times, they don't make sense at all. Their words may sound like poetry, as they link words by sound, not by inherent meaning. They may jump from idea to idea, in what are called "loose associations," or "tangential thinking."

Your task, of course, is to determine if there is an emergency. With people like this, you need to let a little pressure out like opening a valve in a steam pipe. You validate what they have just said, tell them you want to hear more, but before they do, you need a piece of information. You get that piece, let them talk a little more and then do it again, and then again and again.

Figure 24.11 Example: Steam-valving

A call, bizarre as it may sound, might be like this. Notice that how the call-taker shifts tactics when he/she realizes that the caller may be psychotic and isn't responding as one would expect:

Caller. "I hope you can help me! I hope to God you can help me. Worst day of my life. Worse than when my dog died—worse than when my kitty cat and momma cat died."

Call-taker. "Sir, what is your emergency."?

Caller. "Oh, it's bad. Worst than when all the little fishies died."

Call-taker. "Sir, what is your emergency? What is happening right now?"

Caller. "Now is a bad time. Worst day ever—I had a Labrador, sweetest dog, he died two years ago, and this is worse."

The caller continues to talk, babble really, about the pets that have died and how he misses them, but that this is an even worse day.

Call-taker. *(Breaking in and initiating steam valving)* "Sir. Sir! I want you to tell me more about your animals, your very important animals. But first of all, what is your address?"

Caller. "721 Larch Street, two blocks from hell on earth. My sweet sweet dog, three years ago today, she got hit by a car, but this is worse, much worse, much worse."

Call-taker. *(Breaking in)* "Sir. I want to know more about your dog. But first, you tell me, is anyone with you right now?"

Caller. "I'm alone. Maybe I'll always be alone. Nobody is home on Larch Street, I'm alone, my sweet kitty's long dead and my sweet dog is long dead…."

Call-taker. "Sir, you really miss your dog and your kitty, I know that, and I want you to tell me more. But first, you tell me this—is anyone hurt in your house?"

Caller. "I was so sad without my sweet furry dog, and so mad at the man who hit him with his car, I hit my mirror, because I could see the face of the man who didn't save the dog, and…."

Call-taker. "You didn't want to see yourself in the mirror. You broke it. You broke the mirror. Did you get hurt?"

Caller. "There is a lot of red around me. A sea of red."

Call-taker links with dispatch. Sends aid car and police with possibility of slashed blood vessels in the caller's arm.

As you see, *steam-valving* is for the purpose of letting the person tell enough of what is pressuring them internally so that they don't "fight" you for the conversational floor. If you simply demand to know what's wrong or where they are, they may go silent or become more irrational as they perceive your frustration as frightening. You might never know (as in the example above) that they have a severely lacerated arm or other emergency, and have, in fact, called for help. Instead, you would assume that you just received a very odd call from a very ill individual.

Figure 24.12 Rule #7: Steam-valving

This is useful for people whose speech is a cascade of words, ideas, often tangential or delusional. You listen, and then, tactfully but firmly, interrupt. Ask a question or interject a statement, get a response, and then let them return to their cascade of words. Listen a bit, and then interrupt again. Remember, you must show in your response/interruption that you have been listening to what they say.

Figure 24.13 OVERALL REVIEW: Strategies for Communication With People Who Are Having Delusions and/or Hallucinations

If an individual is a psychotic, but always non-emergent repeat caller, the supervisor of the call-center should contact the appropriate law-enforcement agency to set up a discussion with all involved parties on how best to manage this behavior. See Section XI for more details.

If the caller is emergent:
- Threat assessment is the first priority. When a person is fixated on their delusions, listen carefully for dangerous intentions or obsessions. Ask direct questions about what the caller seems to be saying.
- If you've accomplished threat assessment, or you are trying to stabilize them until emergency personnel arrives, listen for the "islands of sanity," the areas where the person isn't psychotic or delusional, and talk about those subjects.
- With few exceptions, don't agree with a person's delusions or hallucinations.
- With few exceptions, don't disagree with a person's delusions or hallucinations, telling them that they are false. Exceptions to the "don't disagree" rule: those with stalking or jealous delusions and those pleading for support while not believing that their hallucinations or delusions are real.
- Differentiate. Don't challenge their view of the world—accept that it is their worldview and move on.
- Steam-valve when pressure is too great.

CHAPTER 25

Welcome to the Rollercoaster—
Tactics for Dealing With Symptoms of Mania

Mania is a state of high energy. Individuals who are manic need little sleep and can be excited, grandiose, agitated, or irritable. They often have flights of ideas, which can be either creative or completely irrational or both at the same time. Their speech is often pressured. Not only is it rapid, but there is a sense that there is more to say than they can get out. They are often extremely confident, and this confidence is often accompanied by a sense of invulnerability. These callers are frequently very selfish and self-involved. They feel so wonderful that their own needs and desires are the only thing that matters. Their judgment can be poor, and they engage in activities that can put themselves or others at risk.

The manic state is associated most commonly with bipolar disorder, in which periods of mania are one-half of a cycle in which the other is periods of depression. Bipolar disorder is also called manic-depression. Some drugs can also cause manic episodes (abuse drugs such as amphetamine, ecstasy, or cocaine particularly), and mania can also be a side effect of psychiatric medications. People with different neurological damage can have periods of agitation that may look very much like mania, but this kind of delirium is often more extreme and disorganized than the classic manic state.

Figure 25.1 Mania Versus Disorganization
If the person is talking very rapidly, but not making sense, and in addition, seems confused, work with them as you would with any disorganized person. (Chapter 21).

Manic people are vulnerable because they are most in danger when they feel wonderful. Imagine the best day of your life. Now imagine feeling that, day-after-day, multiplied by ten or twenty! Can you see how easy it would be to begin to make unwise, even dangerous, choices?

When you feel this good, it seems like a good idea to feel *even better*. Thus, manic people very often want to party. Drugs and alcohol are very tempting, spending money to buy anything and everything you want leads to credit cards run to the max, and the energy often turns sexual and the manic person gets involved with people who may be inappropriate for them or even dangerous.

Manic people often talk in rapid cascades of words, a waterfall of ideas leaping from one area to another. Sometimes you can follow their thoughts, although they are speaking very rapidly, but at other times, they leap and zigzag, making connections that have little or no meaning.

Some manic people become very irritable, and have a hair-trigger temper. They may also be provocative. Rather than their temper manifesting only as reactivity, some will tease and taunt other people. It may seem to be in good fun, at first, but it goes too far—way too far. Others may simply try to pick a fight.

Finally, in extreme manic states, people can become psychotic, with all the symptoms of grandiosity, persecutory, paranoid, and religious delusions that any other psychotic individual might present. Because manic individuals can easily become angry or even violent, it is very important to familiarize yourself with the material on de-escalation in the latter part of this book.

Grandiosity Isn't Confidence

Manic people can act or describe themselves as if they don't have a care in the world. They spin ideas, one after another, and expect both agreement and admiration. They seem utterly self-confident. However, truly self-confident individuals are resilient—unfair criticisms seem to bounce off them. They can respond either with a gracious laugh or a dignified response. Think of manic grandiosity, however, as a fragile structure, like a tower made of spun sugar. It glitters, it glows, and it's huge! Tap the wrong beam, however, and the entire tower falls down in shards.

- If you criticize individuals who are manic, they can experience your criticism as a personal attack, and from giddy happiness, they suddenly turn on you in rage.
- If you try to tease them for their somewhat irrational ideas, or try to joke around with them, they can misinterpret this, too, as an attack. "You are making fun of me!" they yell.

Consider the manic to be in an exuberant hysteria. When they appear happy, it is as if they are on a giddy flight hanging onto a helium balloon. It certainly is thrilling—until they look down! Miscalculated teasing or criticism is experienced as if you are poking at the balloon with a needle.

Humor occasionally can be a useful tool with manic persons. But you need to be calm and centered. You may make a joke that is very funny, but your purpose must be to catch their attention and slow things down, not have fun with them. Trying to match humor with manic callers is like trying to catch a dragonfly in flight. Don't try to match wits with them. Help them slow down instead.

Watch Out—Mania Can Be Infectious

Communicating with manic callers can be very exciting, particularly if they are at low or moderate levels of elevation. They can be brilliant conversationalists—witty, sexy, provocative, and entertaining. It can be like having your own comedian on the phone—fast on their feet, bawdy, and full of fun. We can catch their mood. It is easy to begin to feel grandiose and over-confident ourselves. Hitching a ride on this energy is just as dangerous in the home as it would be on the highway. Once you've jumped in the back seat and are zigzagging down the road at 90 miles an hour, it's pretty hard to get back out of the vehicle. Manic callers assume, when you "hitch a ride," that you are in absolute agreement with them. They merge with you, and assume that what they want is what you want. However, when they instigate an action that you oppose, they can turn on you in ferocious, betrayed anger.

There is an old expression: "He's a drag," referring to someone who slows the party down. In fact, that isn't a bad idea with the manic person. Don't get swept away. Rather, focus on calming yourself, calming them, and calming the situation. It's very hard to get along with someone moving like the Roadrunner in the old cartoons. You don't want your role to be that of the Coyote, chasing vainly after them.

Figure 25.2 Review: Interacting With a Manic Individual

When interacting with a manic individual:

- Remain calm and centered.
- Be conscious of your caller's fragile state of mind, in spite of his/her claims to the contrary. Grandiose doesn't mean strong!
- Don't bluntly criticize.
- Don't tease or joke around.
- Don't join in what sounds like fun. It's not.
- Check with them what their medications are. Have they been taking the meds?

WARNING: Many manic people have poor judgment and a volatile temper. Don't get so distracted by their high energy or the funny things they are saying, that you neglect to do an adequate threat assessment. This can be a caller who is joking and laughing with a dead body in the room.

CHAPTER 26

Interventions Specific
to Elderly People

Remember, older adults aren't a monolithic category. They are people—like all of us—simply older. Everything in this book—every character type, every mode of aggression, every syndrome, and every de-escalation strategy applies to elderly people as well as those of other age groups.

Elderly people certainly can be aggressive, particularly to those involved in their care. Their rage can emerge from dementia, medical conditions, pain, adverse drug reactions, mental illness, and/or any number of stressors.

When speaking with an elderly individual, you should:
- Be aware that elderly people may be resistant to help. This may be due to disorganization, confusion brought on by dementia, by a combination of severe depression and fear, or by pride. ("At least I still have the strength to refuse someone.")
- At the same time, just because someone is elderly, this doesn't mean that they are stupid or mentally infirm. Don't talk to someone like they are a child or feebleminded just because they sound old!
- Speak respectfully, befitting the age and seniority of the person. Too many people speak in a patronizing and demeaning tone to elderly people.
- Call them by the name that they used when they introduced themselves on the phone. If they use their first name, use it. If they use Mr. or Mrs. or Miss or Ms., followed by their family name, use that. If they used both names, choose the family name as default unless invited to use their first name.
- Take time. Of course, in a crisis situation, time is at a premium. Nonetheless, in many calls, a few extra moments can result in a problem solved, rather than an agitated, upset individual who resists help, and may file a complaint later. In certain situations with a very resistant or stubborn individual, you will have to attempt to "nibble around the edges," talking about life, about family. Self-disclosure can be very helpful, once you ascertain that what you reveal about yourself doesn't exacerbate a wound in them, or put you at some kind of risk. For example, "Yes, I have children of my own. Sometimes they don't call. That is really upsetting, isn't it? Now. Mrs. Dennis. What is the emergency right now?"
- Be prepared to become frustrated at the leaden stubbornness, when "the person won't do what is good for them." Remember that what appears as inertia may be a profound expression of fear. Remember also that the most proximate change that many old people are concerned with is

death and therefore, in their confusion or fear, any situation provoking anxiety, evokes the fear of death.

- Don't talk around or about the person to others as if they aren't there, for example, on a three-way call with another family member.
- Don't barrage them with choices, decisions, or too much information.
- Be aware of episodes of rage. Paranoia, whatever the cause, is one of the frequent triggers of rage in elderly people—those with dementia or adverse drug reactions particularly. As the person becomes suspicious, you can often change the subject, so that the object of their suspicion recedes from their awareness. Frequently, the rage and violence that emerges with elderly people is chaotic or terrified. Please refer to Section X.

Figure 26 Elderly May Be Hard of Hearing

A veteran dispatcher pointed out that a number of elderly people are hard-of-hearing. Many, particularly men in her experience, don't like to admit that they can't hear well, and instead, come off as cranky and irritable. The dispatcher noted that the higher registers of female voices are particularly hard to hear, so in such cases, whenever possible, she shifts the call to a male in the room. Sometimes they can hear the lower register male voices easier than a higher pitched female one.

SECTION VI

Suicidal Callers

CHAPTER 27

Suicide and the
Emergency Call Center

Suicide isn't really that complicated a question, is it? If they are expressing suicidal thoughts, send out the police to check on their welfare. If they've made a suicide attempt, send out emergency medical personnel and maybe the police as well. Seems obvious, doesn't it? But it's not.

- Sometimes you have a caller who intends to be the perpetrator of suicide by forcing law enforcement to kill him/her—"suicide by cop." They may be calling about someone else with this agenda. If you miss the warning signs, you aren't able to warn police of the threat.
- Sometimes you have a person who calls, alluding to suicide in vague terms. If you don't know the current level of risk, you may not know whom to dispatch to the subject— police, emergency medical personnel, or both.

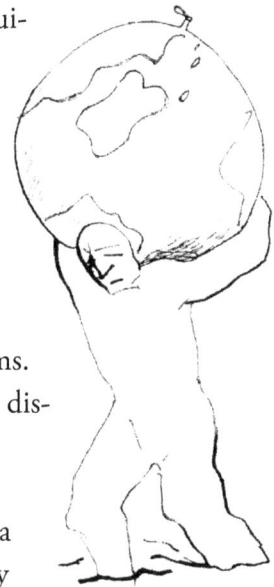

Sometimes they call on a cell-phone and you don't know where they are. All of a sudden, you are filling the role of a crisis counselor, talking to the person as they fade in-and-out of consciousness, or buying time as they press the knife to their wrists, while other personnel try to find their location.

It may be a barricade situation, where the individual called the dispatch center, and continues to talk with you, even with the police at the door.

And often—all too often—you are talking to a repeat caller, who makes suicide attempts or threats on a regular basis, requiring an enormous expenditure of time and money while trying to assure their safety.

A complicating factor is that call-takers rarely know the outcome of a call. It is difficult to grasp the severity of situations that, one after another, seem to ebb away into nothingness.

Figure 27 Experience of One Veteran Dispatcher

Because we rarely hear the outcome, it's easy to become complacent or jaded, especially if we've had received no training on how to talk to a suicidal caller, and the seriousness of some calls can be a rude awakening. I used to think if they are calling, they can't be serious.

I'm thinking of one call in particular: Upon answering the phone with our typical "greeting" which includes "what are you reporting" the caller said he wanted to kill himself. I thought, callously, "yeah, yeah another one." He was cooperative and gave me his address that happened to be in an adjoining jurisdiction. I had one of my co-workers call that jurisdiction while I kept him on the line.

After some random questions including why he wanted to kill himself, I found myself thinking, "If all that was going on in my life, I'd want to kill myself too. What do I say to him now." I floundered around for a few more minutes until someone else came on the line asking who I was. I explained that I was the 9-1-1 dispatcher, and he said he was an officer and would, "take it from here". I moved on to the next call. I found what occurred only because one of our dispatchers knew the officer.

When they arrived on scene, they found my caller holding a chef-type knife to his throat. He'd already cut himself a couple times, obviously hesitating just at the last minute, and it took them an hour to talk him into putting it down. I still wonder if I could have helped more if I had had some training on how to deal with callers of this type.

CHAPTER 28

Suicide as Self-murder—
A Taxonomy

These are questions that we ask ourselves to order our mind so that we can best pass on the situation to law enforcement, EMT or both, a mental tool that can be used to help gauge the seriousness of the person's suicidal threat, and what type of suicide it might be. Given that suicide is a form of murder—that of oneself—then let us categorize it by roughly the same sub-divisions that we do homicide.

- **Aggravated first degree self-murder.** This includes killing oneself in a heinous or torturous way - drinking acid or lye, for example, because the person believes they deserve to suffer. Another example would be a suicide calculated so that a loved one will find the body. A third would be a suicide-murder: killing oneself after killing family members or other people.

- **Premeditated self-murder.** (First degree self-murder) This includes any planned suicide. The majority of the people with whom you speak on the phone will fall into this category. That is why the standard assessment questions in the next couple of chapters are concerned with the suicidal person's plans. Remember this: self-murder is a desperate attempt to solve a problem. The problem of being imprisoned within a situation that one can't escape—one's own life.

- **Second degree self-murder.** This includes impulsive actions, which are due usually to extreme emotion or intoxication. In most such cases, you will be called by a witness, or other involved person rather than the suicidal person.

- **Assaultive self-harm with Intent to commit mayhem.** (First degree assault) In this case, the person doesn't mean to die necessarily, but they do something horrible to themselves, often with the intent to show others, "See how much I'm suffering!" Or "See how much you make me suffer." They sometimes call after they inflict serious harm on themselves.

Figure 28.1 Example: Assaultive Self-harm With Intent to Commit Mayhem

A young man returned home to find his father on the couch having sex with the young man's new girlfriend. He pulled out a fish boning knife and yelling at the two of them and stabbed himself right in the abdomen. Miraculously, the flexible blade threaded its way between his internal organs and all he needed was a few stitches. He later said, "I didn't want to die. I didn't even think of that. It's just that my dad has always done stuff like this to me. Every time I trust him, this is the result. I didn't know how else to show him how upset I was."

- **Assaultive self-harm.** This includes suicidal gestures, self-cutting, and other self-mutilating actions. (Chapter 33)
- **Self-sacrifice.** Rare though it may be, this would include actions that have the intention of helping others—like throwing oneself on a grenade to save one's comrades.

Figure 28.2 Example: Self-sacrifice

A young girl, aged 12, once disclosed sexual abuse by her father, and her mother slapped her in the face for "talking dirty." She suffered it for many more years, but when her father began turning his attention to her younger sister, in the magical thinking of a child, she thought that if she did something as awful as suicide, maybe someone would help her sister. She already knew that disclosure didn't help. Thankfully, her attempt to kill herself failed, and a very good hospital social worker asked the right questions, thereby getting help for both girls.

- **Self-execution.** This includes suicide that is directed primarily by a sense of guilt.
- **Survivor guilt.** This particularly concerns those who have survived a disaster where loved ones or friends have died. A number of those who have served in combat zones feel a terrible guilt when they are able to come home while their comrades were killed or maimed.
- **Mercy self-killing.** This category includes so-called "assisted suicide" or other suicides in which the person is seriously ill and wishes to "die with dignity."

CHAPTER 29

Why Kill Oneself?

Above all else, suicide is a problem-solving activity. The individual, for whatever reason, can't conceive of another solution to their problem. And their problem, above all else, is of feeling trapped in a situation beyond escape. It may be physical pain, business reversals, impending incarceration, or the end of a relationship. The possibilities are infinite. The suicidal person can't conceive of any alternative in which they can exist as a person defined by them as worth being alive.

Figure 29 Examples: Possible Reasons for Suicide

- "I can't live without him."
- "I'm not the kind of person who goes to prison!"
- "I'm going to be held up as some kind of sexual predator just because I told her she was attractive? Now they are going to fire me for sexual harassment?"
- "I've tried to get off dope before. My sponsor tells me that alcohol is a lifelong disease. I guess he's right, because I keep relapsing. What's the point? I'm either drunk or going to some church basement for yet another AA meeting."
- "I have pancreatic cancer. The pain meds don't touch it. It's like you have a weasel inside your belly eating you alive. And the chemo? You take poison and hope it kills the cancer faster than it kills you. I've had it. I'd rather go out now while I still have my dignity."

Problem-solving activity though it may be, it is also the killing of a human being. That it is done by one's own hand doesn't make it a less murderous act. This is an important consideration because, given there is hatred and often a weapon, the dispatcher must consider the safety of the people who will be going out to help the suicidal person. In short, the difference between murder and suicide is often no more than what direction the weapon is pointing.

CHAPTER 30

The Basics of Intervention
With Someone You Believe
Might Be Suicidal

Figure 30.1 Can you say the wrong thing?

Unless you are abusive, callous, or unprofessional, you can't say the "wrong" thing to the suicidal person. The goal is to make human contact to find out what the situation is; to ascertain how dangerous it is; and to keep a link between the two of you while emergency response is on the way.

---

1. **Ask direct questions.** Don't tiptoe around the subject. Vague questions, like, "Are you thinking of hurting yourself?" leave the person an "out." They say, "No, I'm not," thinking, "*Soon, I'll be feeling no more pain.*" How can a depressed or angry suicidal person feel safe in talking to a person who is supposedly expert in dealing with emergencies who can't even talk frankly about suicide?

Figure 30.2 Example: Missing a Suicidal Call

Perhaps you may believe that you always speak directly to your callers, particularly concerning suicide. However, one must always be careful, because some calls may slip beneath the radar. Imagine a phone call from a weeping 13 year old boy who tells you how scared he is because when his father comes home, he's going to be mad, because he took some money from his wallet. Of course, you ask if his father is going to hurt him. And the boy says, "No. He's never hit me. He'll just tell me I did wrong." You may feel very sorry for the boy, but you also think that he'll probably learn a good lesson, and not steal money from his dad again. The problem is that, reassured, you don't think to assess if the boy is suicidal, or *why* he is so upset that he is calling an emergency dispatch center. If you had followed up with the proper questions, you would learn that the father will flay the kid with his tongue, letting him know how useless he is, and how he'd wished he'd had enough sense to have gotten his mom to abort him. Or, maybe the father isn't a bad guy, at all, but this is a very sensitive kid, and one of his friends committed suicide six months ago, and killing himself just seems like a good idea, because then he won't have to face his dad.

The correct question is *"Are you thinking of killing yourself?"* Being asked questions directly is a relief to suicidal people because it indicates that, at last, there is someone who is strong enough to listen closely to what is going on inside them. If the person isn't suicidal, they will let you know.

It won't put the idea in their head if it wasn't there to begin with. **This doesn't mean that you simply blurt out the question at the first opportunity but, if there is any possibility that the person might be thinking about killing themselves, in the proper time, ASK.**

2. <u>**Can you ever ask if the person intends to "hurt themselves"?**</u> Once they have denied an intention to kill themselves, THEN it can be a good idea to ask a follow-up question if the person intends to "hurt" themselves. This enables you to pick up on the people who are either "practicing suicide" or self-mutilating.

3. <u>**Speak in a calm matter-of-fact tone of voice.**</u> If you sound nervous, you'll appear unreliable. If you're too casual, the person will feel that you aren't taking them seriously. If you appear overly concerned, overly warm, or "sensitive," you'll sound like a "counselor"—someone who offers support, but not a person with the steel to take over when that is needed. A calm, matter-of-fact tone shows that you aren't panicked by their situation and that you can handle anything they say.

4. <u>**Act as if you have all the time in the world.**</u> This is a corollary to the above. If you act like there is little time, the person you're talking with will believe you, and they'll rush to a decision or conclusion. (Note: As discussed in Chapter 4, this doesn't mean you take forever to manage the call. This is an attitude – not minutes and seconds on a stopwatch.)

5. <u>**Concerning advice giving.**</u> If you are keeping the person on the line while emergency response arrives, or their location is unknown, don't simply start giving them advice.

Figure 30.3 Concerning Advice Giving

Even when you think you understand the situation, keep advice to a minimum. If you say immediately, "Think of your family," the individual might reply mentally, *"Yeah, they'll be sorry. Their tears dropping on my grave are the best payback I can think of!"*

---

6. <u>**Never dare them to do it.**</u> They may. The kind of stupidity embodied in such phrases as, "If you were really serious, you'd cut your wrists lengthwise, not cross-wise," only works in the movies. People who try to shock another person "straight," are usually fed up, unsympathetic, and really don't care what happens to the caller. They say it for themselves, not the suicidal person.

7. <u>**Don't get in a debate.**</u> Some people use suicidal behavior as a way to feel some personal power in a world over which they have little control. Debates about the meaning of life, the nature of heaven, or the immorality of suicide will break rapport, will aggravate you, and will draw out any negotiations.

CHAPTER 31

The Essential Questions

Figure 31.1 Concerning Police Response

"Suicide" or its variant words demand an automatic police/EMT response in many jurisdictions. The information here is for the purpose of assessing immediacy of risk and what kind of risk the person is presenting. It isn't intended to supersede whatever protocols your agency has in place.

The following are the standard questions for assessing suicide risk. As you can see, there is a progression of questions in which greater specificity indicates greater danger. You aren't expected to be a therapist. You are assessing whether to send out police, emergency medical personnel, or both, doing more assessment and/or intervention while they are en route, or as a part of a longer intervention if you don't know their location (if, for example, they are calling on a cell phone).

Your tone should be calm and straightforward. Given that this is a 9-1-1 line rather than a crisis line, you must be succinct. At the same time, you shouldn't use these questions as a "checklist." You may have to "go with the flow," to some degree, as they may wander off into emotional tangents, particularly if they are mentally ill, or otherwise unstable. Then, you will return to the basic questions.

1. **"Are you planning to kill yourself?"**
   - "NO" If they answer no, follow up with questions and statements why you believe they might. If they can't counter your suspicions satisfactorily ("Your wife called and stated that you told her you were going out in a blaze of glory tonight. And don't look for the body."), then send out the proper emergency response team to assure their safety. If there is even the slightest doubt, send police to do a welfare check.
   - "I DON'T WANT TO KILL MYSELF, BUT I PRAY I JUST WON'T WAKE UP IN THE MORNING." This could be termed passive or soft suicidal ideation. Don't minimize this—the person's pain is very real. Although these individuals can usually be linked with a mental health intervention, either an outreach worker or an appointment the next day, there is still a suicide risk. Your protocols may still demand that emergency responders make face-to-face contact with the caller.
   - "I'M NOT TELLING YOU." If you have collateral evidence that they might be suicidal, send out proper personnel for an assessment. It shouldn't be your job to read their minds. We do need to find out if they are playing games for further follow-up. In severe cases of game-playing, they should incur legal sanctions (Section XI).
   - "YES I DO." First red flag.

> ### Figure 31.2 After the Initial Question
> As discussed above, AFTER you have asked if the person intends to kill themselves and they answer "NO," it is often a good idea to ask if they intend to hurt themselves. This reveals the people who intend to do self-mutilation or are "practicing" to see what a suicide attempt feels like.

2. **"How would you do it?"**
   - "I DON'T KNOW." This, too, means you have time. You should be able to negotiate an agreement to seek or accept treatment. Nonetheless, although such an individual is certainly a lower risk than one who has a plan, there still is a risk. Follow the protocols for dispatch in your area.
   - "I'M NOT TELLING YOU!" More game playing. Respond as above
   - "I COULD DO IT ALL SORTS OF WAYS. (They then give a list.) This is game-playing manipulation—it doesn't mean they won't make an attempt, but their suicidal behaviors are more an "I'll show you!" attitude. Game players may also be showing signs of aggression. Emergency personnel should be alerted to the possibility of suicide-by-cop, or other provocative actions. Please refer to Section XI for discussion of System and Management responses to dishonest, game-playing callers.
   - A CLEAR METHOD. "Yeah, I'm going to cut my wrists. I'll be sitting in a bath of warm water, and I'm hoping I'll just drift off." Second clear red flag, version A.
     OR
   - METHOD AND BACK-UP PLAN. "I've thought of jumping off the Aurora Bridge, but if I don't have the guts, I'll use pills." Second clear red flag, version B.
3. **"Do you have the means to do it?"** (In other words, ask if they have access to the weapon or method that they intend to use to kill themselves).
   - "NO." Once again, that gives us some time. Although even here, we might be able to negotiate them into following up with treatment, or the dispatch of a mental health outreach team, emergency response should, always attempt to make face-to-face contact with such people.
   - "YES." If they are talking about guns or knives, find out if they have the weapon and where it is. Alert emergency response personnel of the potential threat.
   - "I'M NOT TELLING YOU." More game-playing—respond as in previous sections on "game-playing."
4. **"When will you do it?"** This question helps you gauge immediacy, how established the plan is and if there is anyone else who is "timed" to suffer. ("ON MY MOM'S BIRTHDAY").

The more "positive" answers you get to these four questions, the greater the risk of a lethal outcome.

5. **Follow-up Questions.** In most cases, you will have accomplished all that you need to do to establish what emergency response is required. You will know if the individual is or isn't suicidal, and how close they are to the act. In many cases, however, you may have to keep talking: it might

be a barricade situation, or they are on a cell-phone and their location isn't known. The following questions are designed to get more information and to keep them talking. As the individual continues to talk, they'll often pull back on his/her own from their suicidal intention, or become more amenable to de-escalation because they feel that "at last, someone is willing to listen to me."

- "Have you tried to kill yourself before?"
- "Have you ever tried to do it another way?" People get very concrete, and literal. They are only thinking of their current method. They may have made several attempts before, by other means.
- "Has anybody in your family or someone you cared about ever tried to kill themselves?" Such people have "shown the way."
- "Have you been drinking? Using any drugs?" *(Don't push this one if you have a sense that the person will be more worried about getting arrested for use or possession than finding a solution to their problem.)*
- "What's happened that things are so bad that you are thinking about (or planning to) kill yourself? What else have you tried to do to get yourself out of this situation?" *(Be cautious with the second question. The person may think you are about to critique their incompetence at even living. Explain that you are trying to understand so that you don't suggest something they've already tried.)*
- Other areas of concern to talk about include, the individual having suffered any recent losses, being ill, or having little or no social/family support.

With all of these questions, your job isn't to be a counselor or tell them how to be happy. You job is to keep them talking until emergency response personnel can reach them, and/or they discover the strength to pull back on their own.

Figure 31.3 The Important Thing for a Suicidal Person Is Contact

Remember that the suicidal person is profoundly isolated. Just talking to you makes them feel, at least a little part of humanity again. The best intervention is often not the brilliant thing you have said but it is that you were able to keep them on the line—making human contact with them.

CHAPTER 32

The Art of Communicating
With the Suicidal Person

As stated earlier, there will be occasions where you must stay on the line with the suicidal person. You don't have their location or they are barricaded.

- **Don't be a soft touch.** Sometimes the stories that suicidal people tell are heart-rending. Being heart-rending can also be a very sophisticated kind of manipulation. I'm not encouraging cynicism here. I am saying simply that you can feel betrayed or burned out if the person you try so desperately to help spits in your open hand.

Figure 32.1 Examples: Being Used as a Soft Touch

- An ambulance takes them to the hospital and they hop out at the hospital entrance, having used it as a taxi ride downtown.
- You find yourself on the line, feeling that only your voice stands between them and death and then they curse at you suddenly, or accuse you of talking down to them or not caring and then they hang up the phone.
- After all you have done, after talking to them long minutes or even hours, they kill themselves. You tried your best and they are dead. **Remember, unless you acted in an unprofessional or callous manner, you didn't "make" them do it.**

- **Your trust will be abused.** One of the hazards of your business is that your trust will be abused. It is the hallmark of a professional that you don't become burned out because some people were playing games, or playing on a different field than you thought. You have a profession to assess risk and dispatch those who can help. If the frauds and phonies make you cynical, they have won. Therefore, do your best and do it "clean." Even if the other person turns out to be manipulative, ensure that you do your job as a pro.
- **Don't make guarantees of how wonderful life will be.** When the suicidal person makes demands of you, don't give a guarantee of results. Explain the difficulties instead. ("No, I'm not guaranteeing counseling will help. And you will have to work to find a <u>good</u> counselor. Even then, it won't be easy. It might be the hardest thing you've ever done. But it's something you haven't tried.")
- **Don't be a cheerleader.** If you are too active, too "positive," it is as if you are "in it together." Their success will be your success. If you act as if things are *too* important to you, the suicidal person begins to feel that they are doing things for you not for themselves.

- **Don't bolster their "self-esteem."** You may hear that they've got a talent, that they are attractive, or have beautiful children. If you point this out to them, "You have so many reasons to live!"—you will most likely break rapport entirely. It is likely that they know these things themselves.

Figure 32.2 Examples: Not to Bolster Their Self-Esteem

- They look in the mirror and they see their beautiful face, but inside, they feel corrupt and foul.
- They think how awfully they may have been acting towards their children or what a burden they believe themselves to be, and begin to believe that the kids would be so much happier if they were dead. "Sure, they'll be sad for a little while. But it'll be such a relief not to have to care for me. How would you like to be 14 years old and have to help your mother to the bathroom and take a shower and things like that?"
- Yes, they have a talent—they know it—but even as they play the piano or paint or score 27 points in a basketball game, it feels useless and empty.

- **Frame things with negatives.** "You've had a bad time, there is no doubt about that. Yet, somehow, you held it together all these days. What's different about today?"
- **Identify the intended "victims."** Try to ascertain who the suicide is intended to hurt. You will be able to get a better sense if the person is also homicidal, or on the cusp between self-harm and an intention to take others along.

Figure 32.3 Identify the Intended "Victims"

We can often tell if they intend others to suffer based on their answers to such questions as:
- Who will find your body?
- Who will identify your body?

Some people are shocked at the question, so preoccupied with their own pain that they didn't even think that their child, for example, would be the one to find them upon returning home from school. Others describe that same scene with happiness—hoping, thereby that their child will never have a good night's sleep again.

- **Fair witness.** Often, all the person wants is someone to hear them out. They know there is no advice to make things better, but it is so lonely holding the pain.

Figure 32.4 Concerning Being a Fair Witness

One veteran dispatcher stated: "I was on the phone with a barricaded and armed suicidal subject for 45 minutes. I got him to let his wife and baby go. He started telling me about why he was suicidal and it was awful! He got angry with me, saying 'So what do you have for me now?' I said 'I got nothing. Your life really is bad right now and I couldn't handle it. You're doing better than I would.' He started crying and gave up to cops. All he really wanted was someone to tell him that he was right—he was in a really bad place."

- **Internal questions that sidetrack us.**
  a. "I don't know if I would want to live in such a miserable situation." It's not about you. The fact that they called means they still have some hope for another answer or at least someone to hear them out.
  b. "Why is it important that they live?" OR "I know I should care, but I don't." In cases like these, make death itself <u>your</u> enemy. In other words, you <u>will</u> do your level best to speak for life. Not by evangelizing based on some spiritual belief, but by speaking in strong, calm tones, you are, in effect, a voice from the land of the living to one trying to cross over into the land of the dead. If they wanted to die, they shouldn't have called!
- **What if the person is cleaning up their affairs and is calling to tell someone so they don't die alone?** Go with the flow—in other words, you keep them talking, so that they focus on telling their story in a lot of detail. This gives the emergency responders time to get to the scene. Paradoxically, the longer the person talks, the more "human" they usually feel and less likely they are to follow through on their initial suicidal intent.

CHAPTER 33

Self-mutilation

One of the most confusing actions that a person can do, at least to those outside the situation, is self-mutilation. This usually means cutting ones wrists or other parts of one's body, but it can encompass a lot of other actions. Among those I have encountered are:

- Rubbing an eraser on one's wrist until the skin is peeled away and one has a weeping lesion in the flesh.
- Stabbing oneself repeatedly by dropping a knife between the fingers, any error resulting in a wound in the web between the fingers.
- Running a needle in and out of the flesh of one's belly.
- Burning holes in one's face with a cigarette.
- Literally slicing open the abdominal wall all the way to the fascia that holds the organs.

The hallmark of all of these actions is that the person doesn't intend to die, and even in the last horrifying example, where the woman in question cut her torso—a former nurse who uses a scalpel with the skill of a surgeon—she called for help after she made the cuts. There are a number of reasons why someone mutilates himself/herself:

- **Self-hatred.** The individual punishes himself/herself through self-torture and disfigurement.
- **Attention seeking.** These cases are usually typified by superficial wounds. Such individuals "require" others to pay attention to them. The "victims" of the manipulation become afraid that they will be responsible for the self-mutilator's death if they don't act.
- **Primitive medicine.** Like Europeans and Americans a mere 150 years ago, they feel like they are "draining out" the poison by bleeding themselves.
- **A struggle to feel something.** Some people, in the throes of deep depression and/or trauma, feel numb. The torturous acts help them feel alive.
- **Stress reduction.** Physical wounding, like many other stresses on the body, result in the release of endorphins; chemicals secreted in the body that are close chemical analogues to opiates such as morphine and heroin. People can become habituated to endorphin release, and it can become an addictive behavior—one cuts to feel a sense of well-being.

Figure 33 Example: One Woman's Self-Cutting

A young woman stated that after years of emotional abuse by her father—he would leap at her unexpectedly, and scream and spit in her face—"I felt like I was walking on eggs all the time. Then, when my mom finally escaped with me, it was like I couldn't stand any emotions at all, even though I was finally safe. I would be happy, and it would feel like I was going to explode." She described one day cutting herself on the forearm with an "Exacto" knife, and to her shock, felt a sense of warmth and peace—not merely psychological peace but also <u>physical</u> well-being! Several weeks later, she tried it again, and it became an addiction.

- **<u>Rehearsal</u>.** Some people want to commit suicide, but they also want to live. Over and over again, at war within themselves, they make hesitant attempts to harm themselves, and "fail."

How do you triage cases like this? Emergency personnel must respond. Is this something that only law enforcement should go out on? How about a joint response by law enforcement and emergency medical personnel? Is it ever warranted that only the EMT should go out? Remember: The difference between suicide and murder is which direction the weapon is pointing! Best to error on the side of safety.

The way to answer these questions is to ask some. You need to ascertain if this is a suicide attempt, or if they are wounded seriously. You should get as many details as you can on the nature of their wounds, and what they intend to do. Why did they call? What help are they asking for? Just because they overdosed on some pills or made some small scratches on the wrists doesn't mean that you shouldn't check if they have any other weapons or if, beneath the surface of their plea for help, there is hatred and/or rage.

CHAPTER 34

Suicide by Cop

Suicide by cop isn't only dangerous to emergency responders, but also to the public at large. The individual isn't looking for a way out of the confrontation. They are attempting to make the police kill them by threatening to kill law enforcement or other people on the scene. This can be an ostensible hostage situation that turns out to be a "victim taking." In the most extensive study[4] of "suicide by cop" (SBC), the researchers determined that in their sampling, 36 percent of police shootings of males involved suicide by cop. Although the sampling was small, the statistics for women were even more startling—nine out of ten were deemed suicide by cop. There is some debate about these figures—the researchers used an expanded definition of SBC which included spontaneous acts as well as those that were preplanned, but nonetheless, such figures establish that SBC is far more likely than previously assumed. There is no doubt that many armed (or apparently armed) subjects are focused on setting up a situation in which they will be killed; and the easiest way to do this is to threaten to kill someone else. The statistics regarding women are particularly chilling.

Police response, however, is governed by risk, not cause. When an individual points a weapon at a police officer or other potential victim, they must be stopped, no matter what is driving them to act. How, therefore, is information on SBC helpful? It is most relevant in a static, barricaded or apparent hostage-taking situation, where the acquisition of intelligence becomes all important. The majority of individuals enacting a SBC has made a recent suicide attempt on their own, and/or has alluded to the desire to kill themselves, or die. In addition, a substantial number of such individuals have used some kind of intoxicant.

The dispatcher has a special function here. When you get a call regarding a family member or neighbor who is firing shots, or brandishing a weapon, be sure to ask the caller if they are aware of the subject making any recent suicide attempts or statements. Our objective is to ascertain if there is any indication that the individual has been thinking about, rehearsing, or even enacting suicide before today's incident. Any indication of suicidal thinking or action should be forwarded to the officers immediately! The first responders MUST be put on their guard, so that the subject doesn't have an opportunity to force an officer to help them commit suicide.

However, many people, particularly family members tend to lie to law enforcement personnel for any one of a number of reasons. If you ask only if the subject has made a recent suicide attempt, you might get a negative answer. The informant might think they will get the person in trouble, or "they didn't mean it," or "it was a gesture, not real," etc.

Our objective is to ascertain if there is any indication that the individual has been thinking about rehearsing, or even enacting suicide before today's incident. Any indication of suicidal thinking or action should be forwarded to the officers immediately! The first responders MUST be put on their guard, so that the subject doesn't have an opportunity to force an officer to help them commit suicide.

Figure 34 Example: Progression of Questions That Might Prove Useful to Gather Information Relevant to SBC Concerns

Questions:

- "Has Joe made any suicide attempts *in the last two weeks?" Put emphasis in the italicized words, so that the person, if they answer a negative, very possibly will say, "Well, not in the last two weeks."*
- "Okay, not in two weeks. Has he made an attempt recently, then? What did he do?"

If the informant attempts to minimize things:

- "Sometimes people do things they don't mean—maybe to show off, sometimes to figure things out, that only later we think about. Has Joe done anything recently that put himself in danger? Driving too fast? Taking drugs or drinking?"
- "Well, sometimes people say things, maybe they are just thinking them through, and sometimes it's just idle talk, sometimes not. Has Joe made any statements about suicide? How about wishing he didn't wake up in the morning?"
- "Has he been making any unusual decisions recently? Like giving things away?"

SECTION VII

Recognition of Patterns
of Aggression

CHAPTER 35

The Nature of Aggression

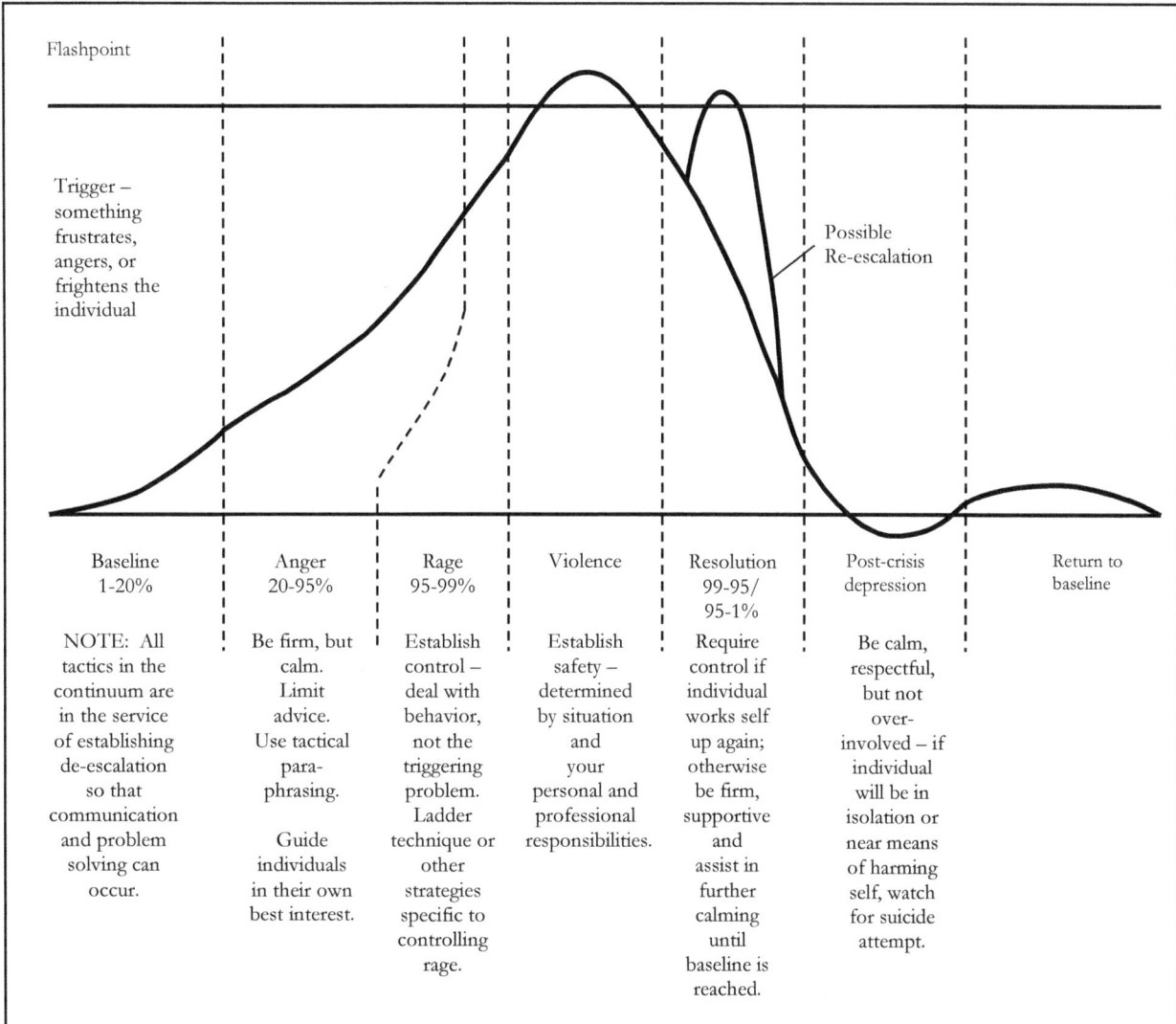

Flashpoint

Trigger – something frustrates, angers, or frightens the individual

Possible Re-escalation

Baseline 1-20%	Anger 20-95%	Rage 95-99%	Violence	Resolution 99-95/ 95-1%	Post-crisis depression	Return to baseline
NOTE: All tactics in the continuum are in the service of establishing de-escalation so that communication and problem solving can occur.	Be firm, but calm. Limit advice. Use tactical para-phrasing. Guide individuals in their own best interest.	Establish control – deal with behavior, not the triggering problem. Ladder technique or other strategies specific to controlling rage.	Establish safety – determined by situation and your personal and professional responsibilities.	Require control if individual works self up again; otherwise be firm, supportive and assist in further calming until baseline is reached.	Be calm, respectful, but not over-involved – if individual will be in isolation or near means of harming self, watch for suicide attempt.	

An outburst of aggression occurs in a cycle that starts with relative calm and ends with relative calm. The aggressive cycle appears to start with an apparent *triggering event*, though, in fact, the crisis may have been fulminating for some time.

Baseline

When we are calm, we are at **baseline**. We use the parts of the brain most responsible for our best human characteristics: thinking, creativity, and human relationships. Let us, somewhat arbitrarily assign this a number rating 0-20. In other words, to be calm isn't to be placid like a cow—we can be energetic, vibrant, even a little upset or irritated, and still think and communicate using the best of ourselves.

Anger

A triggering event elicits a change in both thinking and feeling. It can be something that threatens an individual's sense of safety, infuriates him/her because they haven't gotten what they wanted or desired, or is simply a stimulus that justifies the expression of aggression. The person becomes first irritable, then **angry**. If violence is given the number "100," and baseline is numbered "1-20," then ANGER is numbered 20-95.

Angry people are still trying to communicate with us. Because we perceive their attempts to communicate to be obnoxious, domineering, threatening, or just plain irrational, we often deny that they are trying to communicate. They, on the other hand, experience an increasing sense of frustration or desperation, and not infrequently, a sense of helplessness—even when they refuse to talk with us. This may be because the person feels so angry and frustrated that they don't know how to begin. From their perspective:

- When you don't agree with them, you are resisting what is clearly true or right;
- When you don't seem to grasp what they are saying, you are showing that you are disinterested, too stupid to understand, or your lack of comprehension implicitly accuses *them* of being stupid;
- When you don't agree or comply with them, you are frustrating them in achieving something they want;
- They have a sense of being wronged, most directly experiencing a threat to their "position." Dominance hierarchy, for humans, not only includes one's position vis-à-vis others, but also one's self-image.

As people become more agitated, the areas of the brain that mediate basic emotions take over. At this point, negotiation or compromise becomes less and less attractive. If the person at baseline is eminently human, the angry person is the quintessential mammal. The primary social focus for mammals (dogs, monkeys, etc.) is their place in a pack. It is the same for us human animals when we are frustrated, threatened, or believe ourselves to be ill-treated. That is why angry people use such expressions as "taking a stand," Or "I won't be pushed around," Or "who do you think you are to talk to me that way!" In their increasing frustration, individuals increasingly attempt to dominate you—to "make you" see things their way.

Their domineering behavior is, as much as anything, an attempt to "get through" to you. Think of arguments where you said such things as: "No, that's not what I'm saying! I'll explain it to you again!" or "Let me put it another way!" or "You just don't get it! What do I have to say to make you understand?" We become intense because we want the other person to grasp what we are saying. (This is counter-productive, because we often make less sense when we are angry.)

Anger is accompanied by physical arousal, which functions as a feedback loop to drive the brain toward further arousal. When our heart beat rises to about 10%-15% above baseline due to emotional arousal, we care less and less about the truth. We care about being "right" and proving the others "wrong." Communication is seen as a "win-lose" situation. We interrupt more frequently, cutting other people off, and we listen only to pick out the flaws in their argument.

To deal with or control an angry person, establish *congruence*. This means to "line up" with them so they perceive that you comprehend what they are trying to say. When you line up with the other person, you prove that you are focused on what they are really saying, and thereby also prove to them that they and their concerns are important to you. This, in itself, is powerfully disarming, not only calming them down, but also helping you to actually work together to solve the problem.

Rage

From 95-99 is RAGE. I have deliberately made the numerical rating narrow to highlight that this is a transitional phase between anger and violence.

How can we tell the difference between anger and rage? When someone is angry, you too, may become angered. You might also become concerned, upset, hurt, confused, or frustrated. But unless you are a victim of abuse or you know this person's anger is a *promise* of violence, you are usually not afraid. Why? Although angry people may *later* become violent if they get further agitated, that isn't their current intention. They are trying to communicate with you, albeit dramatically, loudly, or forcefully. At worst they are trying to dominate or intimidate you so that you will do what they want. As abhorrent as this may be, it is still communication. When people are enraged, however, they are, in effect, trying to "switch themselves on" to becoming violent. You get a sense that if they could, they would claw down the phone line and tear your face off. However there are various inhibitors that hold most of us back from violence. The prime inhibitors are:

- **The fear of consequences.** This includes fear of counterattack, legal consequences, social disapproval, or other possible negative outcomes.
- **Morality.** Almost all human beings possess a core set of moral principles where we find in the vulnerability of another human being a "demand" to treat them without violence.[5]
- **Self-image.** For example, a man may see himself as the kind of person who doesn't hurt women, make a public display of aggression, or lose control of himself. These are socialized traits—things we learn as small children, or values we adopt on our own.
- **The relationship.** They feel a responsibility to the other person. Friendship, love, and family hold them back from violence.
- **Learned helplessness.** Some people, abuse survivors, for example, have tried to defend themselves and repeatedly failed. They believe that they can't fight back. The rage, however, is still present inside. We have phrases like "a cornered rat," or "the worm turns," that describe a person who has suppressed their rage, sometimes for years, because fighting back always meant failure, pain, or even destruction. Given enough frustration or threat, such people sometimes explode.

Rage is a set of behaviors, including both physical actions and verbalizations that lessen ones inhibitions so that nothing will hold the person back from violence. They are no longer trying to communicate—they are working themselves up to an attack. They desire to destroy, not become dominant.

What is the difference, then, between rage and violence? Rage is like a rocket ship on the launching pad, right before lift-off. The rocket hasn't moved, but there are flames and steam billowing out with a terrible roar so loud the ground shakes. It is a roiling moment of explosive, tenuous equilibrium. There are only a few moments to act, because the rocket is about to lift off, which is the equivalent of the initiation of **violence**. If you managed to cut off the fuel, even with the flames and smoke pouring out of the rocket, it won't take off. You can still intervene with an enraged person.

Figure 35 The Difference Between Anger and Rage

Imagine someone pulls out a huge plastic container. Through its translucent sides, you can see a dark, hairy shape—a Goliath Bird-Eater, the world's biggest spider. It rustles around, the container shifting in your hands like it is filled with mercury. Is it creepy? Sure it is. Is there any reason to be afraid? Not really. As long as the lid is firmly on the container, you are absolutely safe.

This is the equivalent of anger. Internally you say, "I hope the lid stays on that thing. I'd better be careful how I hold this."

Now, imagine your friend bends down and to your horror takes off the lid. The spider emerges onto the floor right next to your leg. It raises its front legs and opens and closes its 3/4 inch fangs. There is something poisonous, hairy, and mean in the room, and it isn't enclosed in any container! The spider is out of the box. This, metaphorically, is rage.

However, the fear that now arises within you doesn't mean that you are helpless. You can still step on the spider or jump up on a table. A belief that you are helpless is an interpretation, not a fact. Fear is simply the warning cry—the drums at the brink of battle—that demand you *must* act right now.

What you *should* experience in the face of rage is fear. This isn't a bad thing. Fear tells us that we are in danger and that we must do something—NOW! We will most likely be able to handle it, but we had better pay attention. Fear switches us on so that our emergency response systems are activated.[6]

Fear demands attention. A sense of powerlessness, on the other hand, is merely a *conclusion* that some people believe when they are afraid. Imagine two people about to get punched. One feels a sense of helplessness, a crumbling inward. The other feels a sense of outrage and at that instant knows that they will somehow win. That person has an internal sense that even if their body is wounded, their spirit will never be overcome. Fear can and should be a call to arms, not a sign of defeat.

To work with the enraged person, you must establish *control*, a subject I will discuss in detail in Section X. The person's behavior presents an immediate threat to you or others. Control-tactics, be they verbal or physical, are geared to establish the conditions that make the aggressive person no longer dangerous. In essence, using our metaphor above, we say, "Put the spider back in the box—NOW!"

Violence

VIOLENCE is 100 on the scale. Violence doesn't begin when someone is hit or injured. You are in the realm of violence when the other person makes you afraid that someone is about to be hurt—right now. The legal terms for this are "menacing" or "assault." If the person doesn't have a weapon, we are talking about someone who is at about two arm's length distance and further approaching in a menacing way. If the person is violent and has a gun, all the person has to do is point it toward you at any distance. Even if the weapon isn't pointing at you, it is still violence if the person threatens you verbally or implicitly.

Although becoming a victim of violence yourself isn't the main concern of someone working in a dispatch center, it is important to fully understand the aggressive cycle. Violence starts when you have good reason to believe that you or someone else is about to be hurt. Your guiding principle is to establish <u>SAFETY</u>. You do whatever is most effective to protect yourself and the people for whom you are responsible. **Safety is defined by what you must protect—all the people to whom the subject presents risk.**

CHAPTER 36

Why Would Someone Become Aggressive?

Aggression isn't an alien or unnatural emotion. Without a capacity for aggression, humanity would never have survived. Yet what causes more harm to humanity than aggression? For those of us who wish the world and its inhabitants well, it can be a puzzle. Why would someone be swept by rage when it causes so much harm? Why would people be willing to throw away a future, even their lives, driven by emotions that they themselves might be horrified to have expressed even a few moments later?

As you know from your own experience, there are many reasons to become angry or even enraged. We can better control an aggressive individual when we understand what is driving them:

- **Aggression can develop because people are confused or disorganized.** They can't understand what is going on around them or "inside" them due to cognitive distortions or a chaotic situation (too much information for them to figure out). Among those who experience this confusion are those who are mentally ill, autistic, developmentally disabled, intoxicated, or others who are overwhelmed by emotion. At extreme levels, such individuals escalate to *chaotic rage*. (Chapter 52). What is chaotic rage like? Imagine walking in a forest and suddenly a huge spider web drops upon you. You thrash and struggle with all your limbs trying to get free.

- **People feel helpless, enclosed, trapped, and/or overwhelmed.** This is accompanied by a particular anguish. Such individuals perceive someone as the agent of their situation, and they fight desperately to get free from either their influence or their oppression. This sense of desperation could be provoked by being stopped physically from leaving when they want to go, or being in any situation, even spoken words, where they believe that they are trapped.

- **Fear of attack elicited by perceived invasion of personal space.** Every human being has a sense of personal space, a "bubble" within which an outsider is only permitted if invited. If an individual moves inside this space, no matter what their intentions, the other person may experience it as an attack. The "invaded" person then lashes out.

- **A demand for what they perceive as justice.** It is rare that an angry person doesn't believe himself/herself to be justified. Such demands for justice are usually a complex sense of victimization or grievance, and can include:

  a. Individuals who feel that they are losing personal autonomy and power. The person feels dominated and oppressed, and view themselves as fighting for their freedom. It must be understood that this sense of loss of power is personal. It doesn't have to be objectively "true."

  b. Individuals who feel that their rights are either denied or being taken away. Many people experience a sense of violation when they are forced to conform to rules. Whether it is in their best interests or not, such individuals believe that something that is vitally their own is being stolen away.

   c. <u>A "self appointed" revolutionary who is rebelling against an unfair world, system, or group of people</u>. The best sense of power that many people can achieve is in opposition to others. Such people welcome an opportunity to designate others as enemies, legitimizing them as targets for their own anger and hate. Some, particularly those with paranoid ideas, believe that they are being oppressed by systems or powers beyond them. They aren't fighting against inter-personal oppression, but against something they believe to be far larger. If they are aggressive against you, they see you as an exemplar of those larger forces.

- **Intoxication.** A "self-induced" delirium, intoxication leads to poor judgment. For other people drugs and alcohol aren't a "problem"—they are a solution. Alcohol or drugs "liberate" their brutal desires, something observed frequently among perpetrators of domestic violence.

- **Material threats.** People will fight to defend what they have or that to which they believe they are entitled. If a person is going to lose his home or his job, or if he believes that someone is intent on taking something that is his, violence can be viewed as a logical choice.

- **Organic stressors: loss of sleep, fatigue, and insufficient or un-nutritious food.** Brain chemistry changes when the human organism is stressed. This causes changes in perception, mood, and cognition, and among these changes can be an increase in irritability or hypersensitivity.

- **Recent stressors and losses.** Anything that elicits profound emotion can cause the person to become aggressive. This can be the death of someone close, job loss, divorce, infidelity, or feelings of profound insecurity.

- **Entitlement.** For many people, entitlement is intertwined with desire. Their formula of life is that "if I want something, I deserve it, and if I'm not getting it, I have a right to be more forceful so that it is given to me." In short, they think they will get what they want if they just get louder. A sense of entitlement always justifies itself.

- **Ideology.** Religious and cultural factors, be they the larger culture of a society, religion, and nationality, or the smaller culture of a community or family can provide an ideology that legitimizes aggression, even violence. Many cultures offer its members an "operating system" that expects a violent response in certain situations. Furthermore, cultures often define certain individuals as inferior, even less than human. All too many cultures sanction violence against women as a matter of course.[7]

- **Family interactions.** More personal violence occurs within families than anywhere else. There is the friction of arguments regarding everything from house rules to who "owns" the house, irritation due to living too close together, past grievances brought up with no resolution, and a host of other issues. An argument starts, but it quickly degenerates into a demand that each concede that the other is right. Each feels flooded emotionally and becomes more and more frustrated by their inability to "get through" to the other. This becomes all the worse when one or more family member is mentally ill, because what they are arguing about may be irrational or delusional. Families often function as emotional traps—there is no escape from the people who, although loved, cause one the most pain.

- **Romantic relationships.** In addition to all the dynamics described in the item above on families, people in relationships often demand that the other person submit to their wishes. There are numerous reasons to fight, from money to sex to infidelity. The rage is fueled by the same source—"You will love me on my terms," even if the "relationship" is delusional, mere fantasy, or wishful thinking.

- **An individual who has already "given up."** For some, aggression, like its mirror-twin, suicide, is a "problem-solving" activity or a "what the hell" response when one can't find any other solution. Related to this is a person's belief that he/she has no effect on the world. Violence ensures that he/she will make an impact.

- **Hallucinations, particularly "command" hallucinations.** What drives aggression for some people is something "internal, yet external." The person is harried by alien voices—commands that they do harm—the voices asserting an all-powerful identify. The person may feel compelled to act as the voices demand, may become violent in trying to make the hallucinations stop by any means, or may blame others for the presence of the voices.

- **Shame/humiliation.** One of the most powerful driving forces of aggression is a sense that one has been shamed. Shame isn't a mild sense of social embarrassment. It is a sense of being exposed and victimized by others, with no hope of relief. It is a driving force for revenge-based aggression (including stalking) and is also a prime motivator for verbal attacks when the caller associates you, correctly or incorrectly, with someone who shamed or violated them in the past. They may immediately become very angry or brood about it from days to years and then explode into rage, like an underground coal fire suddenly exposed to the air.

- **Person is egged on by others.** This can occur for a variety of reasons:
  a. Some people are set up by others who are amused at getting them mad. The provocateurs, often family members, set up vulnerable individuals out of boredom or for fun.
  b. Other people are provoked by family members or friends who use the person as an instrument of their vicarious desire to inflict harm. For example, a wife says, "I thought you were more of a man. I can't believe you let that neighbor cross our property line without you doing anything at all."
  c. Other people do this to *themselves* by "fronting," making a scene in front of others (friends or family, for example) to increase their status in their "pack." Then they are afraid to back down, because the pack will see their cowardice. Others carry the "audience" inside their imagination, thinking that they must conform to a fantasy of themselves as a fearsome individual to whom others will submit or avoid altogether.

- **Violence as recreation.** Hurting other people is, for some, the most pleasurable activity in their lives. There is a joy in making others submit, and for some, a delight in causing pain. One of the biggest mistakes a dispatcher could make would be to believe that all those who call want help to stop being aggressive. To be sure, most do—that is why they are calling. But the sadistic individual wants an audience, not assistance.

- **Surgical violence.** This is a conscious tactic of intimidation. "I won't hurt you if you do 'x.' If you don't do what I say, I will hurt you very badly." This is criminal aggression, whatever diagnosis the person might have. For example, in a hostage situation, the hostage taker says, "If you do 'x' for me, I will let the hostage go." A call-taker, of course, can't grant anything—you are, in most instances, trying to gather information and buy time until the hostage negotiator can take over. Part of the information that you should strive to gather is to ascertain if the hostage taker is being honest—are they bargaining, or is their "offer" merely part of a game that they are playing with someone who is, in fact, a victim whom they intend to hurt or kill rather than a hostage. The hallmark of the "victim-taker" is that he/she either makes no demands, or the demands are outlandish or irrational. Let me underscore, I'm not suggesting that the call-taker attempt to usurp the function of a hostage-negotiator. It will prove very helpful, however, if you are able to gather any information regarding the barricaded individual's intentions, and chief among that information is if they have a hostage or a victim.

- **Protective aggression.** This is the rage expressed by one trying to protect another person whom they perceive as being victimized. The closer one feels to the victim, the more aggressive the person will be. For example, a caller sees a neighbor harshly disciplining his child, and threatens to beat him the same way he beat his daughter.

CHAPTER 37

What Does Escalation Sound Like?

Ｗhat do people do when they become aggressive? As people escalate, their bodies become activated to posture, to intimidate, to fight, or to flee. Building aggression manifests in a variety of different behaviors.

Mood Changes

- **Nervous, anxious, even frightened.** Such people lash out in defense. They aren't looking for a fight—they are trying to protect themselves.
- **Overwhelmed or disorganized.** Some may speak in repetitive loops, some babble or even though they are on the phone, they talk to themselves. This can be either a manifestation of intoxication or a chaotic mental state.
- **Hostility.** This is the open expression of a desire to harm or intimidate another.
- **Seduction.** This is camouflaged hostility. This is when individuals try to get you to collude with them. For example, "C'mon. My wife was just upset. You know how women are. You don't need to send out the cops—you know that. We're guys here, right?"
- **Erratic mood changes.** This is typified by a rapid shift in mood; for example, boisterous and loud to morose, then shifting from depressed and quiet, to once again, loud—this time belligerent. Such individuals present a risk because they are unpredictable and unable to control their own emotions (Chapter 16).
- **Hypersensitive to correction or disagreement.** Often paranoid (Chapter 17), such people are hypersensitive to other people around them. They may complain of being stared at, watched, or controlled. Hypersensitive individuals feel under perpetual attack. When there is no enemy, they will create one—paradoxically, they don't feel right with themselves unless they discover someone they can accuse of attacking them.
- **Authority issues.** When you try to set limits or say "no," these individuals become very frustrated or outraged, refusing to comply with rules. Limits, in their view, are oppressive by nature. Their motto of life can be summed up in the phrase, "No one can tell me what to do."
- **Electric tension.** This is the feeling you get before a thunderstorm hits. I can't underscore highly enough that you must ALWAYS trust this feeling, the intuitive sense that you are dealing with a dangerous situation.

Cognitive Changes

- **Cognitive distortions.** Negative self-talk that makes the situation seem worse. Such cognitive distortions heighten the individual's belief that they are being abused or threatened.

Figure 37.1 Example: Negative Self-talk

"This will never work out. That dispatcher might promise that the police are coming to talk, but it's open season on people like me."

- **Interpersonal cognitive distortions.** The person hears the worst possible interpretation in what *another* person is saying.

Figure 37.2 Example: Interpersonal Cognitive Distortion

You say, "Ma'am you are yelling too loudly. If I am going to be able to help you, you have to lower your voice." And her response is, "YOU ARE HANGING UP ON ME???!!!!!"

- **Becoming less and less amenable to conciliation or negotiation.** The individual tries dominating the other person, win the argument, or express their frustrations, rather than trying to find a way to a peaceful resolution.
- **Concentration and memory deteriorate.** It becomes more difficult for them to communicate, to solve problems, or to recall past solutions to such problems.
- **The angrier they are, the lower their ability to listen.** They begin to lose the ability to hear the other person's perspective. Only their own ideas and desires have any importance to them.
- **Information processing skills deteriorate.** As their information processing skills deteriorate, their judgment becomes worse and worse: They can't evaluate what is really in their own self-interest.

Figure 37.3 Example: Deterioration of Information Processing Skills

Frustrated that the dispatcher won't send the police to tell the neighbors that they need to cut down their cedar trees because they are aggravating his child's allergies, the angry father yells, "You don't think I'm serious, do you! This is about my kids. You send someone out there right now, or I'm going to start cutting down those trees. And if they try to stop me, chain saws don't only take down tree trunks!"

Words or the Lack of Words

- **Morose, sullen silence.** For the dispatcher, this would likely occur when trying to problem-solve with the caller and they, unhappy with what you are saying, become silent.
- **Cold rejection.** Your attempts to help them with their problem are pushed away.
- **Sarcasm.** Becoming sarcastic. Sarcasm is hostility slightly masked—shaded slightly in a joke or passive-aggressive phrases. They jeer at you, or sneer contemptuously. Their goal is to make you unsure of yourself.

- **Provocative.** They may become provocative, doing and saying things to upset or irritate you. It is a challenge, meant to elicit a response that *justifies* becoming increasingly hostile, if not violent.
- **Game playing.** Playing word games, twisting what you say with the purpose of trying to confuse you or make you feel ridiculous. They sometimes act as if the situation is your fault and that *you* are provoking them. Everything you say is used as an excuse to attack you further. They are setting you up as an object upon whom to aggress, or as an "excuse" to aggress on someone else.

Figure 37.4 Example: Game Playing

The police arrive to find a man viciously beating his wife, and once in custody, he says, "I never would have hit her, but that 9-1-1 operator ticked me off."

- **Becoming increasingly illogical.** Misinterpreting what you are saying. Going off on a tangent whenever you try to offer calming words or a way out of the problem. Others only focus upon one aspect of what you are saying. Ultimately, they become unable to explain what they are doing or trying to say.
- **Becoming loud and demanding.** They become loud and demanding with a belligerent tone, as if trying to pick a fight.
- **Making repeated demands or complaints.** Of such people, we often say, "They have an attitude." The person tries to legitimize a general attitude of grievance by eliciting a refusal to one of their demands.
- **Refusing to comply with rules or directives.** In their mind, it is all or nothing. If they comply, they lose. Only resistance is victory.
- **Using denial.** Totally denying either the facts or the implications of what they are doing. They are so angry that reality is irrelevant. All that matters is that they are right and you are wrong.
- **Using clipped, pressured speech.** Thereby presenting as "over-controlled." It sounds like they are biting their words as they leave their mouth. Such people often use very formal or stilted language. They are trying to present as someone in control even as they have the pent up energy of a volcano. This, like the hypersensitive presentation, is often typical of the paranoid personality.
- **Making implicit threats**—some people do this implicitly when they boast of past acts of violence or warn that they might not be able to stop themselves from doing what they did before.
- **Using abusive or obscene language.** The call-taker's responsibility is to gather as much information as they can from a reporting party in an emergency. <u>Obscenity is an issue only if it interferes with your role in making the scene safe</u>. If remaining on the line with an abusive reporting party is necessary in order to maintain scene safety or to occupy/distract the target, <u>stay on the line</u>. If the situation continues to decline and by staying on the phone, you are able to keep the responders updated to these changes, <u>stay on the line</u>. In either case, <u>don't allow your</u> irritation or outrage at the vile language the caller is using interfere with your professional responsibilities. Only if there <u>is no emergency</u> should you terminate the call.

Figure 37.5 Concerning Vile and Degrading Verbalizations

- You should be concerned with verbalizations that are vile and degrading. The individual's goal is to make you "less than human," thereby giving them license to be aggressive. In their own mind, they might not do violence to a "human," but if you are a _____ (fill in the blank), then it is no more wrong to be aggressive than it would to poison vermin. Their verbal violence against you may be a warm up against a victim or responders to the scene.
- In other cases the obscenities and slurs are a focused weapon. The aggressor uses the words to shock or stun, so that you focus on what they say and miss vital information regarding what they are doing.
- Note, however, that some people use obscenity as adjectives and punctuation. They swear to illustrate their own emotions and ideas and aren't using their words as a form of attack. In the first two cases, you must deal with the verbal attacks as part of their mode of assault. The latter is no concern—if it's expressed as part of an emergency, ignore it.
  a. One phrase that can be helpful in dealing with a frustrated caller who is swearing, "I hear how angry you are about the situation. I'm trying to help you. Let's work together."
  b. Another way could be, "In order for me to assist you in all possible ways, I need to be able to understand everything. I'm going to take a deep breath, and maybe you could too. Then explain the situation to me so I can help every way I can."

The Edge of Attack

Remember the distinction between anger and rage in Chapter 35. The angry person may be trying to dominate or intimidate you. They may be frustrated or very upset, but they are still trying to communicate. The enraged person is trying to remove whatever barriers hold them back from violence.

As people continue to escalate, the risk of violence increases; and they shift from anger to rage, becoming harder and harder to reach. I will present the basic warning signs of rage here. Section X will discuss rage in much more detail, including how best to control and de-escalate the enraged person.

- **Displacement activity.** Hitting, kicking, or throwing objects. This is done to discharge tension, as a threat display and as a "warm up."
- **Scapegoating.** This is a form of displacement activity expressed on living beings rather than objects.

Figure 37.6 Example: Displacement/Scapegoating

A hostage taker, furious with you for not immediately patching in the mayor on the phone, screams at one of the hostages, "Don't you f**king look at me!"

- **Deep breathing.** Those shifting into offensive rage often breathe deep in the chest and down into the belly. This can be slow or fast, depending on how fast their anger is building.
- **Shallow, rapid and irregular breathing.** Those going into defensive rage fearing they will be harmed—usually breathe in a shallow, rapid, and irregular pattern, almost like panting or gasping. Some hyperventilate, breathing so fast that they go into a panic state.
- **Pacing.** Increased pacing, while muttering to oneself, is arousing—bringing oneself closer and closer to the edge or attack.
- **Internalize signs of assault.** Others will internalize all signs of incipient assault, and thus, when it occurs, it seems to appear instantaneous. Right before the attack, these people stop breathing a moment. This is often accompanied by a "quiet"— "calm before the storm." It is as if you aren't there.
- **Berserk behavior.** As the attack is imminent, the person can "lose it"—shaking, yelling, and acting berserk.

Explosion

The crisis will be some form of violent assault, usually physical, but sometimes pure intimidation and verbal violence. After the explosion, most people move to the *resolution* phase in which the individual gradually—sometimes *very* gradually—return to baseline. Their body relaxes, cognitions improve, and their behaviors are less automatic or reactive.

There is often a *post-crisis depression*, partly due to physical depletion (the stored nutrients in the body are used up) and partly psychological. The individual may be remorseful, apologetic, resentful, or merely withdrawn. As a result of their actions, a number of things could have occurred:

- The person might be in the custody of the police, taken to the hospital, restrained on a gurney, or placed in a seclusion room.
- The person may have calmed down, and the crisis wasn't so severe that he needed to be arrested, restrained, or taken to the hospital. See Chapter 55 for a discussion on what to do after the crisis, if the caller is calm enough and you are able to communicate with them.

SECTION VIII

De-escalation of
Angry Individuals

Figure VIII Anger and Rage Each Require Different Strategies for De-escalation

All the techniques in this section concern anger, the part of the aggression continuum that is associated with frustrated attempts to communicate, shifting at higher levels to attempts at intimidation or domination. Some of these tactics work for low to moderate anger (irritation), and others work across the range.

CAUTION: These strategies don't work well with ENRAGED people (discussed in Section X). Using the strategies given in this section with enraged or violent people will likely result in someone being hurt. Conversely, using strategies that are suitable for enraged people with angry people will flame them upwards *into* rage.

CHAPTER 38

Core Principles of Intervention
With Angry People

There is nothing more paramount than establishing safety with any aggressive caller. This means safety for the emergency responders, safety for others within "reach" of the caller, and the caller, too, as best you can. Safety must supersede all other concerns. Everything you say must have a tactical basis—even reassurance or validation is in the service of safety. There are page after page of techniques for de-escalation in the following chapters. Not only are they quite varied; some of them are polar opposites of each other. Some are widely applicable, whereas others may only be useful in very specific situations. Think of them like the scales and octaves of music that must be mastered so that you can improvise freely.

De-escalate First, and Then Problem-solve

Your focus should be on what the person is doing. You can't solve a problem with an angry person. Remember, the angry person sees the situation as a win-lose proposition. He/she will view any negotiation or agreement as a loss of power. For this reason, first eliminate the anger, and then engage in problem-solving.

Trust Your Hunches

Don't talk yourself out of your intuitions. If you have a hunch that something is wrong, you are probably correct.

Be What You Want Them To Be

Embody exactly how you want them to behave: speak calmly, with slow breathing, and logical sentences. You want them to mirror not only your breathing, but also your calm and logic. This isn't an idle wish. People tend to reflect the behavior of the most powerful individual with whom they are interacting. If you are out of control, others will be too. If the dispatcher is powerfully calm, other people tend to become calm as well.

CHAPTER 39

The Tone and Quality of Your Voice
When Dealing With Angry People

De-escalation starts with ourselves: our breathing, our voice, and our physical organization. We must calm ourselves before we calm others. You can say all the "right" things, but if you sound like you are afraid, irritated, or angry, your verbal interventions will have no effect whatsoever and the situation will only get worse.

Firm, Low Pitch

Angry people focus on your tone and react to it more than your words. For example, a bored tone with either impatience or condescension is guaranteed to evoke more anger, not less. When you are angry, your voice will anger others. Try to pitch your voice a little low in your chest rather than your throat. You will feel a little vibration in your chest. This is very important. When upset or frightened, you feel out of control of everything. When you feel the vibrato of your voice in your chest, you get immediate feedback that you have taken back control of your own body—ground zero. In addition, a quiet, but strong, low-pitched voice—only a little lower than normal for you—*communicates* to the other person that you are in control of yourself and the situation.

Slow It Down

It is often useful to speak a little slower than they do. However, don't speak in slow motion or in such a way that they think you are trying to hypnotize them. You are trying simultaneously to get them to resonate with your slower energy and also to keep yourself from being swept up in their agitation.

Not Too Sweet

Unless you are talking to a small child or a developmentally disabled adult, don't sweeten your voice. When you talk to individuals as if they were children—incapable, helpless, or fragile, they will *feel* that way or they will feel that you are trying to *make* them that way. People who feel incompetent believe that they can't make things better. This includes calming themselves so that they aren't assaultive. That overly sweet vocal tone seems to say, "You are a big baby. I don't have high expectations of you. You are too weak, and I have to hold you—mentally—like a child." This can provoke the person to regress to a more child-like state, which can deteriorate easily into hysteria or a tantrum. Others, insulted at what they perceive as condescension, become angrier.

As I stated above, your tone of voice should be strong and pitched low in the chest, conveying the following: "I know this is really hard for you. I can't fix it. But I am willing to see if I can help you fix it yourself."

CHAPTER 40

Working With an Angry Caller

Sometimes an early intervention moves a person to a state of calm. You avert the crisis before it happens. The dispatcher should still get a description of the caller, their full name and date of birth, so police can be sent out quickly, if necessary. The principles below can be applicable with any angry person, but they are of particular value with a person who is irritated—mildly angry.

Assure Them That You Want to Help

As elementary a suggestion as this might sound, simply stating that you want to help can be very powerful.

Figure 40.1 Example: Assurance of Help

A mentally ill woman, very upset, begins swearing at a call-taker, who replies, "Allie, it is absolutely clear that you are upset. Furious! And I am here to help you. But I can't do that when you scream into the phone. I am here to help you with this situation. You can tell me how upset you are. You don't have to yell at me to make that clear."

Demonstrate Empathy

Empathy isn't the same as sympathy, that feeling of sorrow for another person's plight. Empathy means that you grasp, approximately, what other people are feeling based on their physical organization, what they say, and how they say it. Empathy allows you to communicate that you understand their situation; and comprehend their situation, from the inside.

Be Professional

A level of professional distance fosters authority and the ability to control the caller when you must. For example, "limit setting," which is acceptable from a professional, can be experienced as betrayal on the part of a friend. If your voice is *too* friendly or your approach too casual, you won't be able to exert authority when you must.

Find Something to Agree Upon

One of the most essential principles of hostage negotiation is to get the other person to agree about anything.

Figure 40.2 Examples of "Finding Something to Agree Upon"

Two examples:

- "This is a bad situation. But it's not those people's business. Why don't you go inside, sit down, and tell me what's going on. Just because you have a cell phone doesn't mean the neighbors should be listening in."
- "I know you are really upset with what your brother has done. No one should do that to a child. But rather than hanging up, talk to me. Tell me what happened, and I'll be able to help figure out a way to get the situation resolved."

Simpler examples:

- "Will you, at least, think about it?"
- "Does that make sense to you?"

Question to Encourage Thinking

Beyond the requisite questions regarding location and nature of emergency, <u>questions should be addressed only to someone who is mildly upset or agitated.</u> The questions are used to "slow down" the other person to make them think. Ask them what happened to them that got them upset, when did it start, who was there, etc. **<u>WARNING</u>**: Questions don't calm down agitated or aggressive people. Angry people, who are trying to communicate, hear the question as a failure of communication. Your lack of understanding is demonstrated by the fact you are asking questions.

Give Praise for Their Good Ideas

Don't be over-effusive, but highlight any positive moves the person makes. It is important not to feel as if a few compliments will solve everything, but "ride" the praise into a problem-solving solution.

Figure 40.3 Example: Praise for Good Ideas

A person calls 9-1-1 to complain about a property dispute with a neighbor. He is very upset about the situation and like many people, calls 9-1-1 to complain. As the call-taker de-escalates the person and ascertains that there is no threat, the caller suddenly offers his own solution to the problem. The call-taker responds, "I think you can make it work! What you will have to do is talk to the city planning folks. You are absolutely right. This is a zoning issue. It doesn't have to be a personal issue between you and the neighbor. That gets you nowhere fast." Of course, at this point, the caller needs some education on proper and improper use of emergency resources.

Filter Out the Static and Leap Ahead to the Objective

Some callers present a particular problem—"over-inclusiveness." These individuals don't tell you merely what is wrong. They will, in addition, tell you their life story, or voice obsessions and delusions that either have no relation to the current problem or obscure just what the problem is.

Figure 40.4 Example: Filtering Out the Static and Leaping to Objective

"Brandon, I know you need help, but I don't know what kind of help. What is your emergency—*right now?*" You may have to be very assertive, because his delusions or obsessions can be so dominant that he lapses back into them easily. "Brandon, stop. No more about the President. Not now. You are worried about your child. What is the emergency?"

Clarify Misunderstandings

If there is some misunderstanding, you can often avert the argument if you clarify things right away. However, don't try to save face by excusing or explaining yourself.

Encourage More Details

Sometimes, you can't tell, right away if the caller has an emergency. Some people will rush through their explanation, expecting to be cut off. Others are so caught up in the situation that they assume you understand, and therefore, only give sketchy details. Others are so agitated that they don't make much sense. Encourage the person to speak in more detail, particularly if they are so upset that you can't understand what they are talking about. Interject with "We have time. I really want to know what is going on." I am well-aware how busy a dispatch center can be, with phones ringing off the hook and multiple crises happening at the same time. Nonetheless, there are occasionally calls with a hidden emergency that will only be revealed when you get more details. You must "hurry slowly." Your voice is calm and strong and you simultaneously tell the person that there is enough time to talk, but your direct questions to help them focus.

Figure 40.5 Example: Encouraging More Details

You are, of course, not working for a "help-line," which provides para-professional counseling. But imagine that a ten year old child calls, and is talking tentatively about one subject and another, asking you what you do, and when do police go to people's houses, etc. If you hurry him up, he may get frightened and hang up the phone. With the advent of cell phones, we don't always know the person's location. It may only be after the child relaxes and trusts you a little that he asks you what the police do when somebody's grandpa is "doing the bad touch."

Ask What They Think Would Help

This strategy is particularly useful in calls that are unclear. There's obviously a problem, but they aren't happy with your solution, and at least, so far, it doesn't seem like you should be sending out emergency personnel. Ask for *their ideas on what would solve their problem,* and then repeat it aloud "just so I've got it clear." There must be no mockery in your attitude.

- Surprisingly, the angry person occasionally has a wonderful idea on what could fix things. But you sometimes get so involved in problem-solving that you neglect to ask.
- At other times, the utter absurdity of their idea can only be grasped when they hear your reaction. People sometimes get stuck on irrational ideas that they won't let go of until they propose them to another person.

Acknowledge

Try to acknowledge some or all of another's point of view. You don't lose any power when you concede someone is right. However, clearly differentiate where your agreement stops. If you don't, an angry person will interpret your agreement as support for his anger and escalate further.

Figure 40.6 Example: Acknowledge Another's Point of View

"Roger, listen to me carefully. I agree with your complaint about the noise, but I don't agree with what you are planning to do about it. Yes, you *are* right, and therefore, I want to help you. But I don't agree with you that the best idea is to smash their windows so that "one way or the other, the police will come out tonight."

Apologize

In the unlikely event (within this context) that you hurt the other person's feelings, break a promise, or otherwise do something wrong, APOLOGIZE! It won't compromise your authority. It shows that you are a gracious and strong enough person to take responsibility for your own mistakes:

- If the person has a good reason to be upset, or has a legitimate complaint, accept the criticism and apologize.
- If the person is partly right, concede that point, but continue to differentiate where you are responsible and where you aren't.
- However, if someone won't accept the apology or concession, or is making unreasonable demands, don't continue with more and more apologies. If the first apology is rejected, reiterate in a stronger voice: "I meant what I said. I am sorry for what I just said." But if the person continues to berate you, say, "I have already apologized, and I meant it. I can't do it again. James, we have to focus on the subject of your call. Tell me what you are reporting. What is the emergency?"

An Attitude of Calm

An essential factor to lining up with the other person is *your* attitude. Above all else you try to move into the situation with the attitude that **you have all the time you need.** The individual is in an emergency state and believes there is no time left. If you internally agree with them, you are both in crisis, and you won't be able to act as a stable person to help the caller.

Honesty Is Golden

In all but very rare situations, don't promise what you can't do or otherwise try to fool the person. If you suggest a solution to the problem, be clear what the limitations are. The last thing you should do is leave the person feeling betrayed later.

Try to Get the Person to Sit Rather Than to Stand

If you are aware that your caller is pacing and stomping around, try to get them to sit. Physical activity is stimulating, and if angry, leads to more aggression. On the other hand, we associate sitting and talking, with peaceful communication.

Use Tactful Speech

It is very easy to become too familiar or patronizing with people. Be courteous. Your speech, though on the same wavelength, should always be a little more formal than the other person's. Genuinely courteous behavior can often circumvent the aggression cycle from occurring at all. With outraged people, you can be almost ceremonial—"Sir, I realize how upset you are. That's why you are calling. You want to report something about your neighbor, am I correct?"

It is sometimes very powerful to use their family name—Mr., Ms., etc. This formality can, in many cases, change the tenor of a situation. Just as one lowers one's voice automatically when entering a courthouse, many people change their behavior similarly when spoken to on a more formal basis.

When to Use First Names

There are times, however, when the use of a person's first name is advisable. People who are overwhelmed often become childlike, looking for an authority figure to help them. When you call them by their first name, you assume that beneficent authority and the person—reassured that someone is helping them—stabilizes. Sometimes, a hysterical or frightened caller begins to calm down when you start calling them by their first name. Ironically, many people, particularly those up in years, would prefer to be called Mr. or Ms. In a crisis, however, they may feel very reassured when an authority takes over and when called by one's first name, the other seems to be in a protective authoritative role, rather than merely official. However, if the person identifies himself/herself by Mr. or Mrs., or particularly if they are up in years, you may break rapport by shifting to their first name.

Stay Concise and Clear

Use words that are understood easily, and keep it simple—just one thought in a sentence, rather than long run-on, multi-leveled paragraphs. Give two choices, both of which are, in fact, positive outcomes.

Figure 40.7 Example: Giving Two Choices

"It's 4:30—almost closing time. Do you want to call the zoning office today about your property question or leave it until tomorrow? Either way works—you decide."

CHAPTER 41

Paraphrasing—The Gold Standard With Angry People
and Very Often With Mentally Ill People
(Whether Angry or Not)

Paraphrasing is the "gold standard," the most important technique for calming angry or otherwise agitated people.[8] To be sure, if there is an immediate emergency, all you will do is dispatch the appropriate help. But some calls aren't so simple: the individual is confused, terrified, mentally ill, or very young. Unless you stabilize them, you won't even know what their crisis is. Paraphrasing without adding new "stimuli" of your own helps an agitated or confused person organize their thoughts.

An individual's communication often has a number of "layers." Before they reveal the inside layers—what's really going on—they often need proof that you understand what they are saying in the initial layer. If they don't believe that you "get it," they say such phrases as, "You aren't listening to me!" The person, then, will feel compelled to repeat and/or elaborate that "layer" of the problem with more and more intensity. As they get more intense, they often get more irrational and even enraged.

A paraphrase sums up in a phrase or few sentences your understanding of what the person has just said in a paragraph—short or long. If you sum up accurately, you've established that you've "gotten it" that far, so the person doesn't have to say it again. They are far more likely to give you further information or another layer, because they are clear about what you do understand. If your summation isn't accurate, they can—and will—correct you. This is a positive action, unlike answering a question, in which one feels required to explain oneself.

There is another component. For the sake of de-escalation, take a slightly activist approach that is different from simply repeating (mirroring) what they say. <u>Sum up the healthiest aspect of what they have just said.</u> This method is "self-correcting," whereas passive summation can make things worse. For example, if you sum up a person's worst impulses, the other person will find themselves in agreement with you—you have lined up with what is venal or hateful within them. That is the last thing you want to happen.

<u>Remember—they called you, so they most likely do want a resolution to the emergency.</u> On the other hand, if they are, in fact, bent on mayhem, and called just to have a witness to their rage, they will correct you by escalating what they are saying, believing that you aren't getting the message.

Imagine a caller yelling about his daughter. You could simply ask the man what he means, but if he's really upset, you can either *start* with a paraphrase, or *shift* to a paraphrase if questioning doesn't work.

Figure 41.1 "Over the Top" Example: Good and Unskilled Paraphrasing

Angry person. I am so mad at my daughter that I could just wring her neck!"

- **Incorrect paraphrase:** "You want to murder your daughter."
- **Correct paraphrase:** "You are *really* furious with her!"

If you have—using the "correct" paraphrase—accurately summed up the meaning of the angry person's image, they will go on to the next layer:

Angry person. "You won't believe what she did. I come home and find her on the couch lip-locking that punk from down the street, that kid who epoxies his hair in corkscrew spikes."

Remember, if they are talking to you, they are trying to communicate. Therefore, if you are *inaccurate* in your more low-key summation, the other person will correct you with more vehemence.

Angry person. "No, not 'really furious.' I honestly want to loop a belt around her neck and strangle her. Seriously! She better not be home when I get back from here."

Of course, this last reply will require a police response

Why paraphrase instead of asking a question?

The angry person already believes they *have* to make you "get" what they are saying, and a question shows that you don't. This makes them try harder, with even less coherence, resulting in them becoming even more frustrated. They experience failure over and over because they feel they can't get through to you. Once in this state of mind, the angry person feels like they are in a fight, which they are losing. In essence, they experience a question—a demand for an answer—as putting you in a dominant position in regard to them.

Layers of Anger or Agitation

One useful image to associate with anger, or any kind of agitation, is an onion with layer upon layer. However, all that shows at first is the top layer. Paraphrasing enables you to peel off each layer to get quickly down to the core to solve the real problem.

Figure 41.2 Example: Paraphrasing Instead of Questioning

Imagine coming home after a bad day. You are hot, tired, and frustrated. You walk into your house, drop your bags on the floor, sigh loudly, and walk toward the shower. Your spouse says, "Did you have a bad day?" Isn't this irritating? Isn't it *obvious* you've had a bad day? After all these years together, doesn't he/she know when a bad day just walked into the house? On the other hand, imagine your spouse observing you and saying, "Bad day, huh?" You don't have to explain anything. You continue walking towards the shower, and say, "I don't want to talk now. I just want a shower. I'll talk to you later." You aren't "forced" to explain yourself.

Figure 41.3 Example: Paraphrasing With a Mentally Ill Person

Madeline is profoundly psychotic. She calls 9-1-1. As best as you can tell, she is alone. At any rate, she ignores you when you ask to speak to someone else in the house. She says, "There were pink rose petals, rose petals flying all around my head, clouds and clouds of roses." You could ask her lots of questions in order to have her explain what she meant, but instead, you sum up the only thing he understands.

- **Call-taker.** "Pretty confusing, huh?"
- **Madeline.** "You are darn right it's confusing. How'd you like to be in my head?" *(This is the second layer of communication.)*
- **Call-taker.** "It sounds like it must be hard to think."
- **Madeline.** "Hard to think and scary. I fly apart."
- **Call-taker.** "You can't keep things together."
- **Madeline.** "That's when the bad people come."
- **Call-taker.** "The bad people. Madeline, there are bad people there?"
- **Madeline.** "In my head, only. Where the fear is."
- **Call-taker.** "So you are alone. But you are scared by what you see in your head."

Notice the call-taker's last sentence. The call-taker sums up what seems to be Madeline's main concerns, at a deeper level, at the same time, trying to help her orient herself in reality.

By using a few short phrases, you help the person get more stable and convey to you what is really going on. This is far more efficient then a barrage of questions. Paraphrasing saves time.

Figure 41.4 Other Tips for Using Paraphrasing Successfully

- It is very important that your voice is strong. You speak to the person as someone who has the power within to take care of himself/herself and their problem, not as someone who is fragile or volatile (even if they are).
- Sometimes, you can use a dramatic summation: "You are really ticked off!" Here, you sum up the individual's mood with your voice, in addition to what is being said.

Core

We know we have reached the core level when there is no more "progress." The person spins their wheels—stuck, repeating the same issue over and over, with different words, perhaps, but otherwise little change. Some people express relief that someone finally understands what they are trying to say. Others exhibit an intensification of emotion, because you have reached that which is most distressing. When you reach core, and it is clear that you are on the same wavelength, you can begin problem-solving. This can be:

- A summation of the core problem, followed by a puzzled "why?" "I can understand why you'd be so furious at him. What I don't get is why you think that breaking his arm will help you. He gets hurt, sure, but you will go to jail. Why do you want to let that happen?"
- Having validating them every step of the way, you've established that you are a person they can trust. You then can now be quite directive, because people are often willing to accept instruction from people they trust.
- With others, we can engage in a collaborative process of problem-solving, trying to figure out a way to solve the situation that is in the best interest of everyone involved.

Figure 41.5 Author's Experience: How I Learned What Not to Do (The Right Vocal Tone Is Critical)

I was interviewing an acutely suicidal 14 year-old girl in a detention facility. She had witnessed her mother murder her baby brother. Her mother was manipulating her from prison, writing, "I didn't kill him. The alcohol did it. I've forgiven myself. You have to forgive me." The girl told me that she had one wish, to commit a serious enough felony that she would be put in the same prison so that she could take care of her mother. As she cried in front of me, I said softly and gently, like talking to a small child, "It's been really rough for you, huh?" She picked up her head, tears gleaming on her cheeks and snarled, "Tell me something, do all you therapists learn to talk like that in school, or were you born that way?" In essence, she was saying, "I have just told you that I am bereft of a real mother. I have no one to take care of me. How dare you come into my cell, a man I will never see again, and talk to me like you are going to be my new mother?"

I put down my head a long moment, then looked in her eyes and said, "I'm sorry. Can we start over?" It wasn't that easy. It took considerable effort for me to regain any trust from her, although we eventually got enough "traction" to help her get through her suicidal crisis.

What should I have said had I done things correctly? The problem wasn't with my words. It was the tone. I should have looked her in the eyes and said in a strong tone, "It's been really rough for you, huh?" My voice should have conveyed the following: "Kid, this is a terrible situation. It's not fair and it's not your fault. But let's not have any illusions. I can't save you. All I can offer you is a few tools to help you save yourself. It's up to you to pick them up."

Don't Waste It

You won't use paraphrasing all that often. It is a strategy to de-escalate an agitated person who, otherwise, would not be able to organize their thoughts enough so you could help them. Paraphrasing can have an almost electrifying effect with an angry person. Imagine the feeling when you try to pull a splinter out from under your fingernail, and after ten long minutes of struggle, you get a hold of it and pull it out of your nail bed. That is the sense you get when, angry and desperate to be heard, you realize that the other person "got it."

Figure 41.6 Good Paraphrasing Equals Respect

When we treat someone with respect, we aren't trying to make them into something we'd like better, or someone with whom we'd be more comfortable. Good paraphrasing offers respect to the person as they really are.

Figure 41.7 How to master paraphrasing

As you as you view paraphrasing as a 'specialized,' pseudo-counseling technique, you probably won't want to do it—and you won't be good at it anyway. When you are hit by adrenaline, dealing with an angry, perhaps mentally deranged caller, you will stumble over your words if you try to remember to say things like:

- "So what you are sharing with me is . . ."
- "What I hear you saying is . . ."

Don't do this! Many people will find you irritating, and you will be in your head at a time where you must be aware of what's going on in at the other end of the line

You are, in fact, a master of paraphrasing. You do it all the time simply keeping a conversation going, saying things like:

- "Your kid flunked out, huh?"
- "You're not getting a raise."
- "You hate that guy."
- "She's the one."

In short, the natural statements you intersperse in any conversation are perfect paraphrasing. However, because you do this unconsciously, it's hard to tap into as an *emergency technique*. It's easy to perfect, however. Consider this—how many conversations do you have a day? Twenty? Thirty? Forty? <u>In each and every conversation, at an arbitrary moment of your choosing, decide to paraphrase the next thing they say.</u> Just once. Your conversational partner won't even notice. But because you made a conscious decision to do this, your brain notices. That means you have practiced that skill twenty to forty times a day. Consider how good your skill at any physical activity would be if you do twenty, thirty, forty perfect repetitions every day—it would become automatic! Similarly, if you do this every day, you will be able to step into crisis oriented paraphrasing without hesitation. It will be so natural to you that you do not even have to think about it.

CHAPTER 42

Some Guidelines for
Limit Setting

Sometimes you have to draw a line. If a person is misusing the emergency system, or abusive in a situation where there isn't a crisis, then enforce a limit on their behavior. This includes hanging up on them, ensuring that you have an accurate record of their call, their abusive actions, and your response. (Of course, if there is a crisis, one dispatches necessary personnel, even if you don't like the caller.)

If you enable callers who use the emergency system as a solution to loneliness, an anonymous target on whom to vent abuse, or to commit harm in one fashion or another, you have become part of the problem. Limit setting includes:

- Your tone of voice is matter-of-fact. Otherwise, you reveal that they "got to you."
- Inform them what the limit is and then ensure that they understand. This can be a simple statement of fact as to what is required, or whenever possible, offering two choices, either one of which is acceptable to you. They continue to try to argue. You state something to the effect of: "The EMT are on the way. There is nothing more to debate now. You can lower your voice so that we can continue to talk until they arrive, or we can end the call."
- Allow them to save face as long as they are complying. In other words, if they do agree to the limit, they should feel that they are getting something for doing so. An example would be when the person says, "Okay. I will stop yelling. But now I can tell you about what my son did with the car, right?"

CHAPTER 43

Techniques That Don't Work—
The Big Mistakes That Seemed
Like Such Good Ideas

Many of our mistakes are very obvious. As something leaves our mouth, we think, "Uh-oh. I shouldn't have said that!" But some are subtler, and often occur when we think we're doing the right thing.

- **<u>Don't make promises you can't keep.</u>** This won't only be experienced as betrayal, but will also expose you to personal liability.
- **<u>Don't bombard the person with choices, questions, and solutions.</u>** You will overwhelm them.
- **<u>Don't ask "Why?"</u>** There is usually no more unanswerable question, particularly when you are asking why someone is doing something. A "why" question demands that the person "explain" himself/herself, something they may be quite unwilling, or even unable to do. The "why" questions should only be used after you have used paraphrasing to reach the core problem.
- **<u>Don't talk down to people.</u>** This is done deliberately when you feel contempt or irritation towards the caller, or inadvertently when using unfamiliar vocabulary, jargon, or acronyms. Another example would be sighing when the caller is speaking, or talking overly slowly because "they are "too idiotic to understand plain English."
- **<u>Don't use global phrases.</u>** For example, "Calm down" or the kind of scolding that some counselors do, like "That's not appropriate."
- **<u>Don't take it personally.</u>** Don't take it personally when they get upset.
- **<u>Don't scold or boss them around in a demeaning or authoritarian way.</u>** Authoritarian attitudes and behaviors frequently provoke people to anger or even violence. It is true that you, as a dispatcher, will probably not suffer physical consequences. Instead, their aggression will fall on the emergency personnel who will be unaware of how much the person is already flamed up at authority when they arrive. Furthermore, unprofessional or abusive interactions with callers could result in disciplinary consequences or even litigation.

Figure 43 Authoritative Versus Authoritarian

What is the difference between being authoritative and authoritarian? The authoritative call-taker calmly takes charge of a situation, knowing the right thing to say and do, and then carries it out. They are like the army officer who says, "Follow me." The authoritarian call-taker talks down to people; orders them around; and otherwise acts as if they are above the caller. Rather than "follow me," they are like the officer who says, "Go there."

- **<u>Avoid humor.</u>** Although humor, the ability to see a situation from another perspective, can sometimes work like magic in heated situations, it is risky on the phone. The angry person can easily misinterpret this as provocation or discounting of their concerns. It is very likely that the next thing you hear is an angry outburst—"You are making fun of me," or "This is serious. You think this is a funny?" Don't joke in emergencies.

Beware of Self-revelation

It sometimes may seem like a good idea to describe a situation you went through when you experienced something similar such as, fear, embarrassment, anger, etc. Caution!

- That is exactly what the manipulative or predatory individual wants: information about you that he/she can use.
- You can also escalate the other person if they feel you are trivializing their distress. When you say you went through something similar, you can, if not careful, also imply, "And here you are, all messed up while I, with the same problem, am doing fine."
- Finally, if you make a spurious comparison, the person will either blow up or blow you off. Therefore, if someone tells you about the death of their child, you should not try to establish common ground by revealing your pain at the death of your cat.

SECTION IX

A Consideration of Communication With Mentally Ill and Emotionally Disturbed Youth

CHAPTER 44

Talking With Potentially Aggressive
and Mentally Ill Youth

Modern Western culture is unique in its "creation" of teenagers as a special class. In traditional cultures, youth idolized adults because with adulthood came both responsibility and privilege. The creation of a commercialized youth culture has reversed this. Many young people affect an arrogant stance—they assume that they are eye-to-eye, equal with their elders. They speak to adults as if they are peers, and sad to say, far too many adults respond in kind.

Teenagers naturally desire to stretch their wings and feel powerful. They measure power by their effect on others. Making things worse, mass media equates power with violence and the ability to intimidate. Many teens, therefore, see intimidation (which can be everything from violence to such subtle gambits as the "silent treatment," where a teenager makes an adult anxious and over-eager to reach them) as means towards achieving a powerful role in this world.

Many teenagers believe that through aggression they *take* control. At the same time, they experience fear and rage as being out of control. Every time you can deal firmly and effectively with an angry teenager, you demonstrate a kind of power that is at variance to loss of control, something very attractive to teens who may have never seen before.

Youth and young adults show mental illness in much the same manner as adults. If a young person is displaying psychosis, mania, latency, or any of the other behaviors described in Section V, the strategies offered there are fully applicable to teens as well as adults. In this section, I will be describing the character traits that are often related to different modes of aggression in youth. A reader might reasonably ask how one can tell what "mode" of aggression a young person is manifesting on the phone?

View each chapter in this section as a quick step-by-step process. If the approach in the first chapter (Chapter 44) doesn't work, smoothly move on to the next. It is quite likely that you will intuitively grasp that a youth is in one or another mode, and start with the tactics appropriate to that behavior. This section will take things, however, as a step-by-step process. [9]

To reiterate, this section offers information on what approach to take with youth to de-escalate them. Beyond that, specific de-escalation methods for any aggressive person—youth or adult—are discussed in Sections VIII, IX, and X.

CHAPTER 45

No Brake Pads—
A Consideration of the
Impulsive Youth

Generally speaking, the impulsive youth—who is often diagnosed, correctly or incorrectly, with Attention Deficit Hyperactivity Disorder[10] gets angry for the same reasons as any other person, but they particularly get upset when frustrated, or when someone interferes with the gratification of an impulse. Once swept by this anger, it is hard for them to stop. They are often as surprised as anyone else at what they do. They grab something suddenly from a store and run, or in a middle of a verbal argument, take a swing at the person they are confronting. They don't think it through: often they aren't thinking at all.

When trying to de-escalate an impulsive youth, everything you say should be short and direct. Long explanations, empathic response, and so-called "validation" will be ignored—in essence, it won't even be noticed. In crisis, these kids do best with short, firm commands. You help them govern their impulses by <u>calmly</u> telling them what to do.

Figure 45 Review: Dealing With Impulsive Youth

When dealing with an upset or aggressive youth, assume that he or she is in "impulsive" mode until proven otherwise. How would you know that they aren't merely impulsive or upset? If the following strategy doesn't work, go on to the next strategy. Remember, we are talking about an approach that takes only a few moments—this isn't a counseling session!

- Give them firm, brief commands.
- Help them regain control by directly telling them what to do.

CHAPTER 46

Conduct Disorder—
Fierce Youth

The fierce youth displays calculated aggression. They usually know what they are doing. If they shift into a rage state (that phase right before violence), it is typically in one of three major categories: fury, manipulation, and predatory behavior—topics discussed in Section X. At least while they are in their aggressive mode, these youth often seem to be without conscience. Adults who display the same characteristics are referred to as "psychopaths."

Fierce youth strive to defend themselves against any need for other people, as well as building up a callous attitude in which they extinguish caring for other's pain. It is a mistake to try to establish an "empathetic" connection with such callers, particularly when they are enraged. In possibly causing them to let down their "guard," empathy is experienced as an attack. With limited human ties, pride is their most important "possession," and they will live and die for it. <u>This pride can be considered an access route for communication and de-escalation.</u> The formula, therefore, is "respect outweighs sympathy." Respect means, in this case, that you take them seriously, not approvingly.

Enforce rules with calm gravity and strength. Let them know what you are doing, and where they stand with you and with the "system." Never ingratiate yourself, or try to prove you "care," as this will invite contempt. If you show yourself to be a strong individual who doesn't make the conversation "personal," you have the best chance of dealing with them.

Figure 46 Review: Dealing With Fierce Youth

You first approached the youth as if their aggression is impulsive and you tried to exert authority over them. That didn't work—instead, the youth becomes more focused and directed in his/her aggression towards you.

- Respect before sympathy! Don't try to prove you care.
- Deal with them on a professional, slightly disinterested basis.
- Let them know where they stand—that anything you are enforcing isn't "personal." You are simply doing your job.

CHAPTER 47

Dynamite Under a Rock—
Explosive Kids

These young people can carry a variety of mental health diagnoses. It also includes youth with head injuries, fetal alcohol spectrum disorders, and other neurological problems. The hallmark is that they can be normal, but they sometimes "lose it." When something sets them off—usually a personal affront—they shift into "hot rage" (Chapter 51). They *know* what they are infuriated about, but they can't let it go. Unlike the impulsive kid, simple commands don't calm them down. Imagine a fire so hot that anything—even the blanket you throw over the blaze—is new fuel that allows the fire to simply burn hotter.

If you ever deal with such a youth (or adult) on the phone, your task is to not get flamed up yourself and use paraphrasing, a technique that is described in detail in Chapter 41. You sum up their mood, thereby proving you got the message. They don't have to "deliver" it any more. If it isn't a life-threatening situation, you are essentially trying to contain them until they can calm down themselves. You are helping them "burn out." It is the equivalent of putting them alone in a room or the back of a squad car to cool off–it you give them no fuel, there is less possibility of a fire.

Figure 47 Review: Dealing With Explosive Youth

You are dealing with a young person and attempted to exert authority, and then, when that didn't work, you tried professional respect and distance that you use with the fierce youth. When the youth continues to ramp upwards into further aggression, assume you are dealing with an explosive youth. They get more and more aggressive as if they don't have a "circuit breaker" that helps them turn off. They become very reactive to just about anything you say or do.

- Don't get flamed up, no matter what they say (which will be pretty bad).
- Use paraphrasing (Chapter 41).

CHAPTER 48

Even If You Force Me,
I'll Still Make You Miserable—
Oppositional-defiant Youth

Now diagnosed as oppositional-defiant disorder (ODD), such kids were once called "brats," or "spoiled." Dictatorial parents, who try to break the child's will, often "create" oppositional kids among those who are too strong-willed to crumble. Their motto seems to be, "You won't break me. Even if you make me do it, I still say 'no.'" Other parents who aren't consistent nor enforce coherent reasonable discipline (too permissive or chaotic) also elicit such behaviors. Here, the child is implying, "I will act out until you are forced to give me some limits."

However, even youth from solid homes display this type of behavior. Our culture, supported by a toxic media and advertising world, endows youth with special status. Couple this with a focus on "what my friends are doing," and alcohol or drug use can result in the development of youth with "attitude."

Oppositional-defiant kids are incredibly argumentative, fighting over fine-points, as well as claiming to not be understood. This isn't a search for truth or equity—it is simply a power tactic. Frustrating and defying adults becomes its own reward, and they get a grandiose sense of their own importance as they do so. However, they are contemptuous of adults who take this seriously. It is important for the adult, perceiving this tactic, to disengage, and refuse to participate in fruitless bandying or argumentation.

Dealing With Oppositional-defiant Youth

You are dealing with an aggressive youth. You attempted to exert authority as you would with the impulsive youth, professional distance and respect as you would with the fierce youth and not adding fuel to the fire as you would with the explosive youth. None of it worked. The oppositional kid <u>doesn't want to calm down</u>. The fight is its own reward. With this young person, you will either cut things off, if it isn't important, or <u>revert </u>to firm, undeviating authority.

- Choose your battles. Don't get distracted by side-issues that the oppositional person (youth or adult) throws out as gambits just to keep the conflict going.
- If it is a situation that is important, be dispassionate, calm, and undeviating. In other words, "this is what you will do, there is no argument here, and no discussion either." And <u>don't</u> react when they argue. Simply tell them again. Your attitude and voice should be as firm and indisputable as gravity.

Figure 48 Review: Dealing With Oppositional Youth

- They believe they've won if they anger you or get you upset.
- Don't argue; require them to follow your instructions. Be like gravity.
- Pick your battles. If they aren't worth arguing about, disengage.

CHAPTER 49

Pseudo-Nihilism

It is probable that you will deal with such a youth in a suicide situation—it is also conceivable that it will be a barricade or hostage scenario. On occasion, they call on behalf of a friend, but even here, they often act like they don't care about the situation.

Such a youth, who may affect a posture that includes boredom, self-destructive behaviors, or pretended disinterest, is striving for power "through the back door." They try to make themselves outcasts, because their sense of power increases when they can horrify, disgust, or offend others. Taken further, they achieve power when they experience themselves as untouched by other people or our larger society.

One is most concerned about youth of this type by what they hide inside. These kids, in particular, need an adult to be a "fair witness" to their world, able to provide feedback in a way that he/she doesn't feel compelled to resist. They need someone with more life experience to talk with. Don't be emotionally bland when you speak with them. Instead, pay close attention to them, and offer them a human reaction. At the same time, you must demonstrate that you don't *need* them to change their character—just their actions in this moment. Even in the heated moments of a 9-1-1 call, you may be the only adult who can provide this or has provided this in quite some time.

Figure 49 Review: Dealing With Pseudo Nihilism

This youth is cut-off. Their primary goal seems to be to NOT make a link communicating with you. Other youth may be very much at odds with you. They may even rage or curse at you. More commonly, they treat you with contempt.

- Don't try to make them change or "feel better" by telling them, for example, that they are young and these things pass, or they have a lot to live for, etc.
- They may try to repel you with what they say, or say they have done. Give them a human reaction, but not an over-reaction.
- Be the adult that they almost surely don't have in their life.

SECTION X

Managing Rage
and Violence

CHAPTER 50

Preface to Rage

Rage and anger aren't different only in degree. They are different modes of being, just as water, once past the boiling point, becomes steam. Angry people posture to establish dominance or to force compliance. If nothing else, their goal is to communicate what they are feeling. Enraged people, on the other hand, are in a "threshold" state, trying to disinhibit whatever is holding them back from the ultimate expression of rage—violence. Therefore, all the strategies described in the previous section in dealing with the angry person are more or less useless against those who are enraged. Let us note, however, that we arbitrarily assigned anger within a scale of 20-95. This is a very broad range of arousal, ranging from mildly irritated to truly inflamed. Rage is 95-99, with a peak of 100—violence. Taking into account then, that these numbers are images rather than scientific measurements, we still may use some of the de-escalation strategies for anger when the person is at "93." However, past a certain point, the enraged person is intent only on committing mayhem. Their focus is how to overcome what is holding them back: fear of consequences, damage to their self-image, and/or innate morality. Their internal restraints are "fighting" a battle inside them with their primitive desire to maim and destroy.

Figure 50.1 Author's Experience

As one man who had been in a manic psychosis told me later, "You came into my room and I decided to kill you. I was just about to make my move, and a voice in my head said, 'You aren't allowed to kill him. He's your friend.' I couldn't remember exactly what a friend was, but the voice said, 'I don't care if you remember. It's against the rules to kill your friend.'" Fortunately, aware of his hair-trigger tension, I left his room, perhaps saving my life in the process.

Rage is an internal war. <u>Our task is to control the situation *and* the other person so that their inhibitions are strengthened.</u> In this sense, what we refer to as "control" is actually supporting the inhibitions within the enraged person until they are able to stay peaceful without that imposition of control.

There are various types of rage. It is very important to recognize what type of rage the person is expressing, because we have different strategies to deal with each type. At the same time, don't worry that you will have a lot to remember. Enraged people's behavior is quite obvious—after reading this section, you will easily be able to tell what type of rage they are in, and will know the best strategies to use to control them.[11]

Figure 50.2 CAUTION!

Here, and in several other areas of this book, we have used animal symbols to aid in the understanding of various types of rage or other behavior. For example, we use the image of a leopard or a shark in describing predatory rage. These are thought devices, and are not intended to be used in either paperwork or communication to describe such individuals. In our hypersensitive times, such a reference to a specific person may be misconstrued as stigmatizing them as "being an animal." Nothing could be further than the truth. The images are to assist in understanding modes of behavior, not character. Nonetheless, such images should remain aids of understanding, not terms of reference.

CHAPTER 51

Hot Rage

When we think of people on the edge of violence, it is hot rage that comes to mind most often. We imagine ourselves facing someone, probably a man, with muscles writhing, yelling or screaming, fist brandished and threatening, intending to harm us—now! They throw things, tip over desks, and spit in our faces. They want to beat us bloody, stab us, or pound us into a pulp.

Theory

Think of hot rage as a combination of primitive drives and trained actions. Such "pseudo-instinctual" behaviors are actions that have been either repeated so often or are so ingrained by early powerful experiences that they function almost like reflexes. The person in hot rage, however, isn't totally out of control. For example, an enraged street fighter swings wildly, doing his best to knock his victim senseless, but he also keeps an eye out for the police while he's attacking. *Think of a grizzly bear or wolverine—shaggy, fanged, and clawed. They will tear right through you to get what they want.*

General Information About Hot Rage

Among the various types of high level aggression, hot rage is most frequent. This individual desires violence, and their actions are attempts to get past whatever holds them back from that violence.

- **Emotional arousal.** This mode is typified by emotional arousal or excitement.
- **Deterioration in judgment.** Over-arousal leads to deterioration in judgment, and at higher states of arousal, even basic cognitive processes. The enraged person falls back on pseudo-instinctual behaviors that function, to some degree, automatically. An example would be a domestic violence perpetrator who grabs the phone from his wife's hand and smashes her on the head with it, with the dispatcher listening.
- **Lack of guilt and concern.** Hot rage is often a behavior that has gotten a person short-term success in the past, such as scaring and beating a selected victim so that they are broken psychologically. Such a person has no concern about longer-term consequences, and experiences little guilt.
- **Arousal breed's arousal.** The more enraged people become, the easier it becomes to be violent.
- **Sense of liberation.** For some people, there is a sense of liberation, even a paradoxical kind of joy when they peak into rage. All one's fears and insecurities disappear. For this reason, some people desire rage, because it is, to them, the best thing they ever feel.

- **Displacement.** Displacement is common: Instead of hitting you (yet), they hit an available target like a chair, wall, or other object. This also includes picking things up and slamming them down, or throwing things. They are trying to discharge tension, intimidate their victim and also "warm up" to attack.
- **Domination.** Hot rage is also associated with primitive attempts to dominate an individual or a group.
- **Frustration.** It is sometimes claimed that hot rage is a result of frustration, but this emotion alone doesn't elicit rage in normal people. It is when frustrated desires are coupled with something "personal"— when one believes oneself to be blocked by another person in getting one's desires met that the person becomes enraged.

De-escalation of HOT RAGE: The Ladder

The primary method of de-escalation for hot rage is called "The Ladder." It is used only for rage—that gray zone between anger (even extreme anger) and violence. The enraged present an immediate danger to someone, and unlike the angry person, is no longer trying to communicate with you. The person is right on the edge of assault—in a sense, doing a war dance to eliminate any inhibitions which hold him/her back from committing what he/she most desires—violence.

The Ladder is only effective right before, during, and after the peak of the crisis. Almost all your callers are angry, VERY angry people, not enraged. If they are angry, even extremely angry, you should use the kind of tactics I described in the previous chapters, not the Ladder. Control tactics will provoke rage in an angry person, whom we may have over-estimated due to their loud tone or dramatic behaviors. Remember the image in Chapter 35—is the spider in the box or out on the floor? The difference is that the danger is NOW, not merely something possible if the situation continues to deteriorate. You are attempting to calm and control them so that they aren't a threat to others in close proximity or to emergency responders when they arrive on the scene. You are attempting to calm them down so that you can communicate with them on the phone. The general hierarchy of danger, from most to least, is as follows:

1. Brandishing a weapon at someone;
2. Approaching someone with menacing intent;
3. Pounding or breaking objects;
4. Pacing or stomping;
5. Shouting/screaming;
6. Vile language that is intended to violate, demean, or degrade.

The technique itself is simple. Start with the highest level of dangerous activity that you are aware of. Give the aggressor a straightforward command to stop that activity. Use a short sentence with no more than four or five words. Repeat it. Repeat it again. After a couple of repetitions, always add, "We'll talk about it when you…." Choose the most dangerous behavior and demand that it cease. NOTE: Don't use "psychologese," like "It's not appropriate for you to…."

Once the dangerous behavior stops, go to the next level of problematic behavior and use the same technique. Continue until the person is de-escalated. By keeping things simple, don't get distracted with "why," or other questions unanswerable as the person shifts into rage.

You should frequently intersperse your sentences with their name, using this to pace and break the rhythm of your commands, as well as "calling them back" to a human relationship, name to name, person to person. People on the phone often fluctuate between rage and anger. If they sustain the rage state, they often throw the phone or slam it down. If they are talking—screaming actually—this means that they are still striving to find a way out of the situation. Therefore, once you get them to stop the screaming and verbal assaults, you will shift into any of the number of communication tactics described in previous sections.

Figure 51.1 Example #1: Ladder Technique When the Rage Is Directed at Someone Near to the Caller

They are on the phone with the dispatcher:

Speak at a slow, strong pace. Although the words on this page are spaced close together you use timing, breaks in rhythm and changes in volume, and tone to "grab" their attention. The dispatcher says:

"Darnell, put the gun down and talk with me. Put the gun down. Put the gun down. Darnell, put the gun down. You and I can talk when you put the gun down."

"Darnell, stop hitting the walls. Okay, it's not the walls, stop hitting whatever it is. Stop hitting things, Darnell. We can talk when you stop hitting things."

Darnell, I can't hear you when you are stomping around. *Notice the paradoxical communication, you may be able to hear him just fine as he walks around the house. When you say this contradictory statement, however, you have a chance to "catch" their attention as they try to figure out the sense of what you said. This draws in the higher areas of the brain—the part that tries to think through a problem, taking into account long-term consequences. Once re-activated, the person is likely to be less assaultive.*

"Darnell, sit down and we'll talk. Sit down, Darnell. We'll talk about it when you sit down."

"Darnell, lower your voice *(See below. The second example can also function as a continuation of this episode.)*

Figure 51.2 Example #2: Ladder Technique When the Rage Is Verbal and Directed at the 9-1-1 Dispatcher

Speak at a slow, strong pace. Although the words on this page are spaced close together, you use timing, breaks in rhythm, and changes in volume and tone to "grab" their attention:

"Lower your voice. I can't hear you when you yell that loud. Lower you voice and we will talk." *Notice the paradoxical communication; of course, you can hear a shouting person loudly. (See the first example for a fuller explanation of paradoxical communication.)*

"Talk to me with the same respect that I talk to you. We will talk about it when you stop swearing. Stop swearing. Mr. Parker. We will talk when you talk to me with respect, the same way I talk to you." (*Remember don't worry about swearing as punctuation—like, "My f-king car got broken in!" It is swearing that has the intent to violate you that needs to be address as part of the Ladder.*)

NOW YOU SHIFT.

"Sir, you are really upset. I got that. I'd be upset too if I found my car broken into. Mr. Parker, I am listening. Your car was broken into, and they not only stole your stereo system, but they also trashed the car as well."

Work your way down the "rungs" until the person is no longer in a state of fury –THEN, you problem-solve with them.

Remember, the Ladder should be used only with an enraged individual. Using this technique with an angry individual, even an extremely angry person will cause them to flare up in rage.

Figure 51.3 Concerning Hot Rage

The other primary reason to recognize the hot rage state is to alert emergency personnel as to what they will soon be dealing with face-to-face, particularly if you weren't able to calm them down on the phone.

CHAPTER 52

Chaotic Rage—A Consideration of Rage Emerging From Various Disorganized States

I discussed disorganization in considerable detail in Chapter 21. This chapter concerns the disorganized individual when they flare up into rage. Individuals who go into a chaotic rage are usually suffering from a confusion of thoughts and perceptions. They are disoriented, often experiencing severe hallucinations, illusions, and/or delusional thinking. Chaotic rage is common as part of a variety of syndromes, typified by profound disorganization of cognitive and perceptual processes, including severe psychosis that has "crossed over" into a delirium state, mania, drunkenness, intoxication of various drugs, drug withdrawal, severe intellectual/developmental disabilities, senile dementia, and a variety of inflammations or lesions of the brain. <u>Unlike a classic psychosis, the most salient characteristic is that it is almost impossible to establish a line of communication with the person.</u>

These individuals often can't string their thoughts together logically: uttering cascades of words making no sense whatsoever, or grunts, moans, or mumbling. Others make sentences based on rhymes, puns, or cross-meanings. They may laugh or babble, without any clear object, or completely out of proportion to the possible humor of the situation. The individual may speak in repetitive loops, becoming stuck on one subject, which could be real, hallucinatory, or so much a manifestation of their disorganization that you don't even know what they are talking about.

People in chaotic rage states can become quite frightened or irritable. They may begin yelling, screaming, lashing out physically, and engaging in such self-injurious acts as scratching and gouging their own flesh or head banging. <u>Any state of chaotic rage should be considered a potential medical emergency.</u> De-escalation, in whatever form it takes, must be followed by medical attention as soon as possible. The delirium state, in particular, can be a sign of a life-threatening emergency.

Disorganized individuals enter into chaotic rage states when they are frustrated, confused (too much stimulation), or feel invaded (when an EMT, for example, tries to check the person's responsiveness to light or to stimulation, things that he doesn't understand and wishes to resist). They can be simultaneously enraged and terribly frightened. Impulsive and unpredictable, their rage sometimes explodes, seemingly out of nowhere. Think of TAZ, the cartoon character in the Bugs Bunny cartoons.

People in a chaotic rage state strike out in all directions—they aren't coordinated, but nothing—no fear of injury or consequences—holds them back from their attack. They may grab, scratch, bite, kick, and strike in flailing blows. They are often indifferent to pain or injury to themselves. They may think that everyone—visible and invisible—is after them. Some disorganized people do target people to harm—combat with them is like fighting a tornado of arms and legs. Others are so "lost" that they aren't fighting, per se. They are "swimming through people." It is as if they are drowning in a flood, the people and objects around them the wreckage they are trying to forcefully swim through. Some people in chaotic rage states, particularly trained fighters, retain their coordination even though they are completely "gone" on a cognitive level.

The call-taker will rarely be communicating with a person in a state of chaotic rage. More often, you will be responsible to recognize from another caller's information, that the person is potentially or actually in such a state so that you can correctly inform emergency personnel to be prepared.

Verbal De-escalation of Chaotic Rage: When a Chaotic Person IS on the Phone

Although it is unusual, there are times when a chaotic person does get on the line: perhaps most common are the severely intoxicated, but your caller could also be in a medical crisis.

- Use a slow calm voice, with a firm tone. Your voice helps them orient, not only physically, but as an emotional touchstone as well.
- Delirious or intoxicated people are both impulsive and unpredictable on a moment-by-moment basis. Try to get information from collateral contacts regarding any triggers that set them off in the past.
- Particularly if they are initiating an action that is dangerous to themselves or others, try to distract them and then redirect them to another activity.
- They often use *confabulation*, making up stories that they then believe, as a means of trying to appear normal and stabilize themselves. In exceptional circumstances, you can sometimes "confabulate" a theme yourself that catches their attention and seems to engage higher thought processes, delaying their outburst of rage until help can arrive.

Figure 52.1 Example: Confabulation—Chaotic Individual on the Phone

You are on the phone with a chaotic individual. His wife has called, saying he's been binging on meth for five days, and that he gashed himself with a knife, and is raving about cutting Satan out of their child. He grabs the phone, and begins screaming incoherent phrases. Emergency response personnel are on the way. You are trying desperately to keep the person on the line, and not focused on the baby. Among the words he is screaming, you hear a question—"Angel? Angel? Are you there?" Although I have written previously about not "agreeing" with delusions, this is a terrible emergency and an exception. You say, "Yes, Tony, it's me. It's Angel." And you begin saying whatever you can to keep his attention on you until the police can get to the house.

- One of the last things we "retain" is our name, so use their name, repetitively, interspersing it frequently in your commands in order to get their attention before initiating attempts to redirect them to another activity.

- Do whatever you can to minimize environmental stressors. In a situation that isn't immediately dangerous, where you are communicating with care-givers, tell them to dim bright lights, diminish noise, and "settle down" the environment. Tell them to turn off the music—unless it's keeping the chaotic person calm, and to clear the room of onlookers or extraneous personnel.

- While communicating with the chaotic person, use simple, concrete commands with no more than a single "subject" in each sentence. Several repetitions are almost always helpful. Use just one thought at a time, as complex sentences will be confusing, and thus threatening or irritating. For example, say slowly, "Sit down, William. Sit down. Sit down. William, sit down."

About "Excited Delirium Syndrome"
(See Appendix 1 for Protocols Specific to Excited Delirium)

Excited delirium is a rare condition at the extreme end of the hyper-aroused wing of the delirium spectrum. Etiology can be varied, but it is most commonly associated with long-term use of stimulants: particularly cocaine and methamphetamine. Single doses of such drugs as PCP, pyrovalerones such as methylenedioxypyrovalerone (so called "bath salts"), and very rarely, psychedelic drugs such as "magic mushrooms," can cause chaotic rage states. It is also associated with extreme manic or psychotic excitement, and can be precipitated by a variety of purely medical conditions. It is typified by some, if not all of the following: a sudden onset of extreme agitation; pervasive terror, often without object; chaotic, sudden shifts in emotions, disorientation; communication difficulties, including screaming, pressured incoherent speech, grunting, and irrational statements; aggression towards inanimate objects, particularly shiny objects like glass and mirrors; hyperarousal with unbelievable strength, endurance, and insensitivity to pain; hyperthermia accompanied by stripping off clothes; and most notably, violent resistance to others, before, during, and after arrest or restraint.

Accompanying their almost unbelievable level of physical arousal and resistance to both physical and mechanical restraints is respiratory and cardiac arrest. <u>These people die!</u> The usual pattern is that they struggle with incredible power and then, suddenly, they stop moving. Or sometime after becoming quiet, either in a stupor or in seeming normality, they die, usually from cardiac arrest. This can look remarkably similar to a seizure, also a very dangerous syndrome.

Whenever you receive a call concerning an individual showing some or all of these behaviors, get both police and an emergency medical team on scene now! If you recognize, from the caller's description, that the subject might be in an excited delirium state, your system (law enforcement, emergency medical technicians, hospital ER) should already have a plan of action to deal with such individuals. Your responsibility will be to initiate the plan, by informing relevant personnel that a person presenting these behaviors has been contacted, and summoning *both* police and emergency medical teams to be on-scene. <u>Correct protocol demands that EMS should be staged, and ready to intervene medically the *instant* the individual is physically subdued.</u>

Such individuals can be appallingly dangerous both to others and to themselves. <u>I can't emphasize strongly enough that this is a medical emergency manifesting as physical danger, and usually requiring police and emergency medical intervention to secure them so that they can be treated.</u>

Figure 52.2 Concerning Excited Delirium

Most individuals who go into chaotic rage <u>aren't</u> in an excited delirium, but given the ever-increasing abuse of stimulants (methamphetamine, cocaine, etc.) that are the main precipitants of this condition, it is important that you are familiar with the signs, and symptoms of this syndrome. The call-taker, in almost every case, merely gets the information that an individual is displaying some or all of the behaviors enumerated above. The dispatcher contacts both police and EMS and informs them that the subject of concern is very likely in an excited delirium state, based on a report that they are displaying some or all of the behaviors enumerated above. This alerts the emergency responders of a) the extreme danger of the situation; and b) the need to activate the proper protocol to keep themselves and the subject safe.

NOTE: What if you inform the emergency responder that the individual may be in an excited delirium state and they respond, "What's that?" In such an event, your response should be as follows: "The description I got was of someone delirious—completely out of it. Like he's on PCP or huge amounts of meth—I'm calling out emergency medical personnel to stage on-scene so that they can intervene the moment the individual is in custody. The information I received sounds like a combination of a dangerous, potentially assaultive individual, and a medical emergency at the same time. I don't want the officers to be put in a position where *they* have to try to keep him alive while they wait for EMS to arrive—so they will be on scene, ready to move in when it's safe."

Figure 52.3 Excited Delirium or Chaotic Rage?

Most individuals who go into chaotic rage aren't in an excited delirium, but given the ever-increasing abuse of stimulants (methamphetamine, cocaine, etc.) that are the most common precipitants of this condition, it is important that you are familiar with the signs, symptoms, and "best-practice" interventions. Furthermore, we strongly urge local law enforcement, emergency rooms, paramedic organizations, and 9-1-1 dispatch personnel to become fully familiar and trained to deal with individuals suffering from this syndrome. A joint training of all who may be involved in the restraint and treatment of such individuals is imperative. You need to have an established protocol to ensure public safety, law enforcement safety, AND the safety, as best as you can accomplish it, of the delirious subject.

Greater knowledge about this syndrome has led to a new problem. Because excited delirium has finally begun to be recognized by the medical community as a genuine medical syndrome, this complicates things for both first responders and 9-1-1 dispatchers. Most of the terms in this book, such as psychosis or disorganization, unlike schizophrenia, are general terms. Therefore, they are usable by non-medical personnel. They are descriptive rather than diagnostic terms.

- However, if you use the term excited delirium, you might be accused of diagnosing the person. Therefore, I recommend that you use the term **Chaotic Rage** to describe such individuals, because it is fully descriptive, encompassing both the disorganization AND the agitation that such individuals display. Furthermore, neither the dispatcher nor the first responder is required to make a distinction between a person with genuine excited delirium from a mushroom intoxicated naked man running down the street from a distraught grief-stricken individual in a chaotic state. All parties, from police, corrections, EMS, and dispatch can use this descriptive term without running the risk of being either over-specific or diagnosing in the street.

This term will help officers, on a behavioral basis, to distinguish Chaotic Rage from either lower levels of disorganization or psychosis so that best practice interventions can be used.

Figure 52.4 A Career Ending Experience

I am aware of one incident in which a law enforcement officer's career was ended by such an individual who grabbed hold of his arm, and yanking as if he was cracking a whip, not only dislocated the officer's shoulder, but ripped through all the ligaments of his shoulder and shoulder blade.

Catatonia: Special Considerations

This is a very rare, very bizarre condition in which a person stays in a fixed, immobile posture. People, of course, may not move for a number of reasons, including injury, seizure, or shock. The possibility that they might be catatonic, however, adds some special concerns.

Unlike mere immobility, catatonia is caused either by mental illness (schizophrenia) or an organic condition (drug toxicity—Ketamine and PCP both can provoke this condition). The individual is fixed in a posture that would not be congruent with injury or seizure. Often the posture is quite awkward or twisted. A classic symptom of true catatonia is "waxy immobility." If someone else moves their body or limbs, such people maintain the posture into which they are moved. These individuals will often be totally unresponsive to sounds, touch, or even pain.

Considerable caution is needed in dealing with immobile individuals for several reasons. First of all, they may be injured or having a seizure and at medical risk. For this reason, a medical evaluation is *always* required.

This condition is profoundly dangerous to others as well. These individuals should be viewed as exerting 100 percent of their will to <u>not</u> communicate with the outside world. Trying to help, police or EMT might be tempted to try to get them to respond when they are unrestrained. This can be a disastrous mistake. Imagine the incredible exertion of will required to maintain immobility for hours, even days, without movement, without response, without even blinking in some cases. Now imagine disturbing this equilibrium. The individual shifts in to *catatonic rage*, a form of excited delirium, from 100 percent quietude to 100 percent explosive motion.

Whenever an individual is immobile and unresponsive, of course you will summon medical attention. Inform medical staff and law enforcement of any signs of immobility and unresponsiveness—they might be in a catatonic state, something that can only be determined on the scene. <u>Such cases should be viewed as potential Chaotic Rage states, with much the same protocols</u>. If the individual stays catatonic, then law enforcement's responsibility will be to be on "stand-by" in case the person explodes, and to assist in restraining them on a gurney, if added personnel are necessary. If they do shift into catatonic rage, then subduing the person as quickly as possible is the standard protocol, in order to assure everyone's safety.

De-escalation of Developmentally Disabled Individuals: Special Considerations

De-escalation tactics aren't remarkably different with developmentally disabled folks, but one must be aware of their cognitive deficits. If you use language that is too sophisticated, either in terms of meaning or nuance, you may elicit more frustration and anger within the person. You will be making them "feel stupid."

<u>Speak to them at their emotional age</u>—small child, young kid, pre-teen, or teen. Most of my associates and I have found within a short time of speaking with such a person, we can quickly estimate their "emotional age," by listening to their tone of voice, and their choice of words.

Finally, one can still use Paraphrasing (Chapter 41) with an enraged developmentally disabled person. In this case, however, don't just sum things up calmly. You will use an almost dramatic voice, over-emphasizing words. "YOU are REALLLLLY mad. You are SO upset about your dad!" Your voice is a combination of drama and enthusiasm. The angry or enraged developmentally disabled person finds themselves in an interaction where, despite the energy, there is no "fight" coming from you. In a different situation, you can use the same communication style with someone who is disappointed or unhappy. "Wow. You REALLY loved that puppy! I KNOW that. You really, really wanted to take care of him!" Your dramatic voice validates how important the situation is to the other person and it is the voice, here, more than the words, that provides that validation.

CHAPTER 53

Terrified Rage

What does terrified rage sound like?

These individuals believe that they will be violated or abused. Their voice can be pleading, whiny, or heartbreakingly fearful. They usually breathe in short gasps, panicky, fast and high in the chest. When they yell, there is a hollow quality, as if their voice has no "bottom." This is due to the tightening of their abdomen and diaphragm, so that not only their breathing, but also their speech is high in their chest. They may yell, almost screaming, such phrases as: "Leave me alone! Don't let them in here! I will hit them! You keep them out!"

What causes terrified rage?

Severely frightened people often suffer from paranoid delusions, a fear of the unknown or terrifying hallucinations. At other times, they are afraid of a loss of control, of being laughed at or humiliated. Some people are afraid that they are in terrible trouble with some agency—be it police or mental health professionals. This is a frequent manifestation of post traumatic stress, a condition that arises not only on the battlefield, but also as a result of abuse and violence in the home. Please note that there is no "veteran's rage" or post traumatic stress disorder (PTSD) rage." In-stead, the combat veteran may express hot rage, chaotic rage, terrified rage, or predatory rage. Nonetheless, among these various modes, terrified rage is among the most common responses to threat among the traumatized. *Imagine a wolf cornered, backed up against a cliff face.*

De-escalation of Terrified Rage

Not infrequently, the caller who shows terrified rage is mentally ill or simply very young. If they are a child or childlike and aren't in danger that things would get worse if someone in the house found out they were talking to you, ask them if they have a dolly or a favorite toy. Tell them to hold the toy and continue to talk with you. You can repeat such phrases as: "You hold onto that dolly. Hold onto her so she won't get hurt. Hold her tight." You are subliminally suggesting that you are "holding" them the same way.

Your basic goal is to reduce their sense of danger: Your voice is firm, confident, and reassuring.

Figure 53 Reducing the Sense of Danger
Keep up a reassuring litany of phrases, speaking slowly, with pauses—like this:

"I know you are scared.————I know, you don't want to hurt anyone.————Put down the knife.————You don't need that.————I'll help you keep things safe without a knife.————You can put it down now.————I'm way over here on the phone.————Just listen to my voice.————I will help you keep it safe.————The police are coming soon, so I want you to put down the knife.————You don't need that.————Okay put the knife back in the kitchen. Then come back and sit down and talk with me some more."

DON'T say, "I'll protect you." Many people who go into terrified rage have already been hurt by people who said that kinds of phrase. But when you say, "I'll help you keep it safe," you are bonding with the person's own desire to protect themselves."

As they calm down, their breathing will get a little shuddery or be expressed in short high-pitched gasps. Although you won't see it, they will often slump into a chair or the floor and even begin to weep. Keep up with your reassuring litany.

CHAPTER 54

Predatory or Cool Rage

This type is like a panther or a shark. They are cold intimidators who threaten with vague innuendoes or explicit threats. Their threats are delivered in cool, dangerous tones, often *after* a clear and strongly stated demand. They offer you a chance not to be injured if you comply with their demand. A variant tactic is to pretend to be out of control. (They are "in control" of their "out of control.")

These individuals have developed the application of cold rage as a deliberate weapon of terror, or even enjoyment. Paradoxically, their physical arousal is often low. Their heart rate can go down as they prepare to commit violence. They can be charming and attractive, like fictional pirates. Therefore, some people may have a hard time believing that they are so willing to terrorize others psychologically or physically hurt others, because they can pretend to be such nice people. They are the type of people who can con a law enforcement officer in an alleged domestic disturbance that no violence or sexual abuse happened. The predatory individual lacks a moral sensibility or conscience. They have nothing inhibiting their aggression other than tactical calculation or self-interest. They have no capacity for sympathy or guilt, and many experience extremely low levels of anxiety in situations that would frighten ordinary people.

De-escalation of Predatory Rage

This is simple. It is a crime to menace a dispatcher. Contact law enforcement immediately, so that the caller may be properly dealt with. Your other responsibility when receiving a call, either from the predatory individual or from another individual about the predatory person is to document their menacing threats accurately, so that emergency response personnel know exactly what they are approaching.

CHAPTER 55

The Aftermath—
What to do now?

Rage and even more so, violence is an exhausting experience—both emotionally and physically. Many people get the "shakes" after such an incident. So much blood has "pooled" inside the core of their bodies to prepare them for combat that they feel cold and start to tremble. What is almost universal is a post-crisis fatigue, a combination of the depletion of energy stores in the body and the cumulative effect of all the mood and cognitive changes previously described.

It is likely that you are familiar with the feeling of post-crisis depression. Circular Breathing (Chapter 8) is one of the best ways to mitigate such an emotional crash. It is a lonely experience if you become isolated in the aftermath of a disturbing call, one that particularly evokes a sense of fear, helplessness, or anger. Getting a "fair witness" (Chapter 5) can be invaluable. Whenever possible, discuss the situation with a colleague or another person whom you trust.

In addition, be as realistic as possible concerning your ability to have solved the crisis situation from your distant position at one end of a phone line. Hold onto your sense of self as a worthy human being, doing the best you can. Ultimately, that's all you have.

CHAPTER 56

Conclusion

Y ou may wonder why there isn't a chapter on violence. It's simple. If they are talking to you, consider them to be in a rage state. Violence is when they are doing things—terrible things—to other people or themselves. This is the responsibility of law enforcement to stop. If a person is presenting with rage, you will address some or all of these in the following order:

1. Quickly determine the mode of rage and use the interventions outlined in this chapter best suited to deal with that mode.
2. Start with trying to get them to put down or disarm any weapon.
3. Try to get them to move away from any possible victims.
4. Try to get them to stop any displacement activity—hitting or smashing objects.
5. Try to get them to sit down.
6. Try to get them to lower their voice.
7. Try to get them to stop using abusive/assaultive language.

If you are successful thus far, you will now shift into some of the strategies in the earlier chapters appropriate to dealing with angry or mentally ill people. Of course, along with this will very likely be instructions on how to comply with law enforcement or emergency medical personnel who are en route.

Now that you have finished the front-line portion of this book, you have really just begun. You should become as familiar with this information as you are with the information necessary to drive your car or use your telephone. Just as you snatch your hand away from a hot stove, or blink your eyes when a small object flies toward them, these skills must become so familiar that they become automatic.

Even for some of us on the front lines, it can be profoundly difficult or aversive to consider the subject of potential violence, particularly to the innocent, but is most realistic and helpful to all to prepare for the worst. Such skill will create the greatest possibility that other's aggression and the distortions and confusion of your mentally ill callers will be something you control on the line.

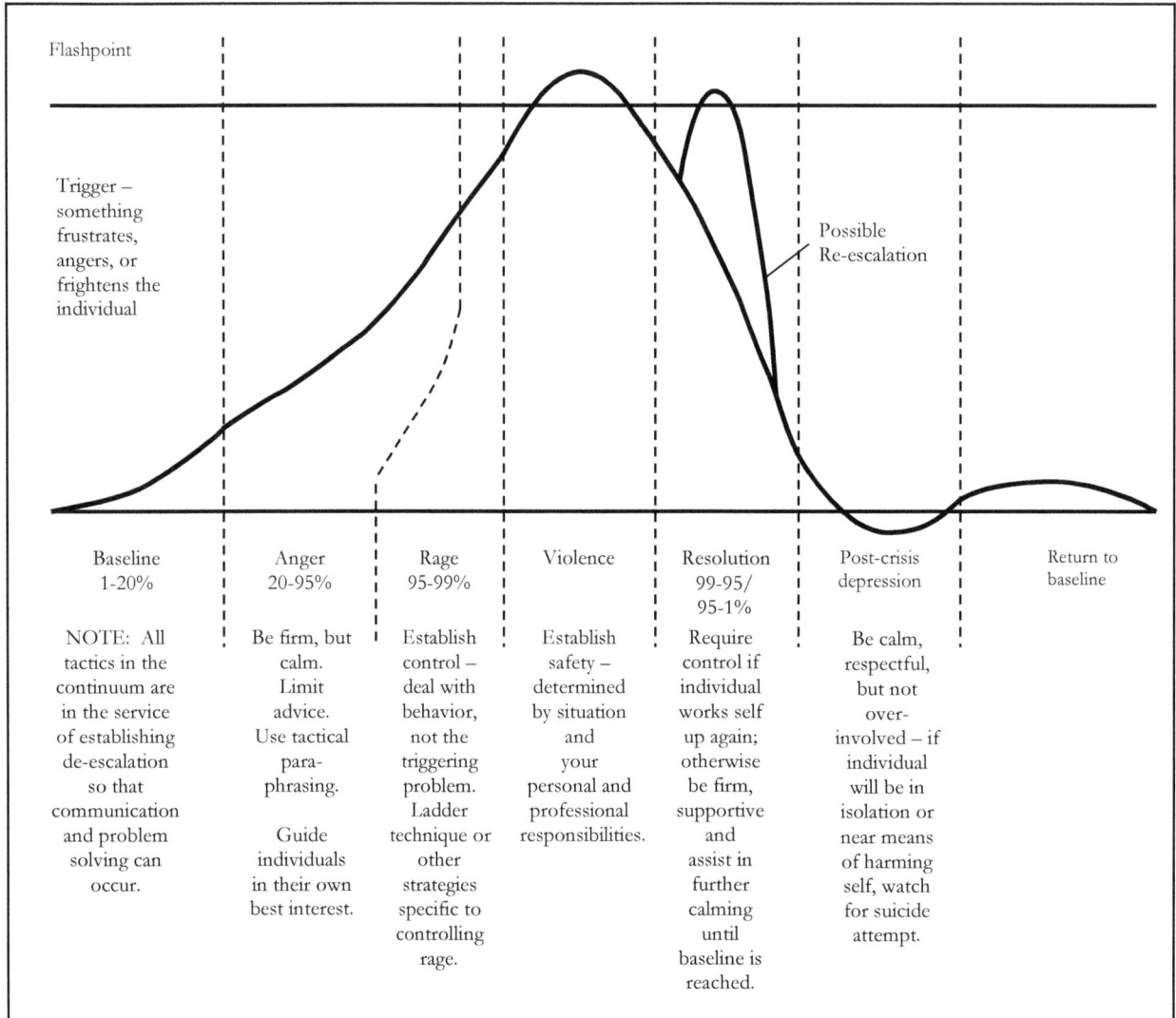

Baseline 1-20%	Anger 20-95%	Rage 95-99%	Violence	Resolution 99-95/ 95-1%	Post-crisis depression	Return to baseline
NOTE: All tactics in the continuum are in the service of establishing de-escalation so that communication and problem solving can occur.	Be firm, but calm. Limit advice. Use tactical para-phrasing. Guide individuals in their own best interest.	Establish control – deal with behavior, not the triggering problem. Ladder technique or other strategies specific to controlling rage.	Establish safety – determined by situation and your personal and professional responsibilities.	Require control if individual works self up again; otherwise be firm, supportive and assist in further calming until baseline is reached.	Be calm, respectful, but not over-involved – if individual will be in isolation or near means of harming self, watch for suicide attempt.	

Flashpoint

Trigger – something frustrates, angers, or frightens the individual

Possible Re-escalation

SECTION X

Management and Systems Issues

CHAPTER 57

Establishing a
Culture of Safety

The Essentials of a Strong Call Center

Professionals are people who are so suited to the vocation they have chosen that the job itself is its own reward. The development of professionals is most likely to occur when management has established an ethic in which safety and security are paramount. Some of the following items may seem far from immediate instructions on how to deal with a disorderly or aggressive person on the phone, but if an emergency call center isn't grounded in such basic principles, staff has nowhere to stand. Elements of a sound foundation include:

1. **Care.** If staff doesn't believe they are being taken care of (adequate safety, benefits, pay) resentment and anxiety will increase, no matter what administrative procedures and rules are in place. Employees who must focus on day-to-day survival have far less energy to devote their full attention to their callers.

2. **Job Security.** If staff doesn't have a sense of job security, resentment and anxiety will increase, no matter what care they receive. Of course, no one is guaranteed a job for life. Nonetheless, when staff trusts that management and human resources will take into account such things as out-placement, job-search, or other counseling when an unavoidable staff reduction is necessary, they are far more committed to the well-being of the organization itself. Enhancing job security engenders a sense of reciprocity, where employees are committed to the well-being of the organization and its members.

3. **Power.** If staff doesn't have a sense that their work and ideas count, resentment and anger will increase, no matter what "security" they have. "Power" means that employees have a voice. Staff members are actual stakeholders in the organization—not only do they matter as generic employees, but they, as individuals, matter too. If people have concerns or ideas, they know to whom to speak, and they also have assurance that what they have to say will be given due consideration.

4. **Respect.** If staff doesn't have a sense that they are treated with respect and dignity, resentment and anger will increase, no matter what "power" they have. "Respect" is an even deeper sense of empowerment, which includes accountability. Staff are given responsibility and held responsible for what has been given.

5. **Protection.** If staff doesn't have a sense that they will be supported by management when they deal with aggressive or complaining callers, resentment and anger will increase, no matter how "respected" they feel. Beyond the more vague precepts expressed previously, staff must know the agency is working proactively to ensure their safety. This includes the following:

a. Management supports staff when they set limits on verbal violence and harassment, whether it comes from callers, outsiders (family members, advocates for a caller, etc.) or even other staff. Staff must know that their concerns won't be minimized. Instead, the agency as a whole, will gather its resources in the best interests of both staff and callers.

b. As difficult as it can be, management must have the courage to strive to rid the agency of those who have become obstructionists to the greater good, i.e., rumor-mongering, being loud or abusive to callers, etc.

c. Staff has confidence that new hires will be vetted fully regarding their past history, and that if staff members present any risk to anyone, they will be retrained or terminated, as the situation warrants. Simulation training is a great way to enhance the vetting process.

6. **Consistency.** Consistency is a key component of any agency that works with emergencies in regards to rules and discipline. With all the stresses of the job, any deficit in this regard will quickly lead to a deterioration of morale and performance.

7. **Voice of experience.** Seasoned dispatchers can teach life-skills—both job related and in regards to the larger world—to the younger or newer members. The strongest organizations are those that foster mentoring relationships. When this isn't done, a group often devolves into cliques, with older employees and younger employees separated into two groups. When each newer employee has a mentor, they have someone on the front lines to give help and advice that they might not feel comfortable discussing with management or human resources.

8. **Good policy.** Not only must the policies be fair, they must be predictable. In an ideal world, staff must be able to assume that the rules will be the same tomorrow as they are today. However, in many call centers, the rules change on a monthly, even weekly basis. It is essential therefore, that management ensures that changes in policy are well-posted and well-explained.

9. **Adequate staffing patterns.** Without sufficient personnel, everyone will be on edge. Staff members will be concerned that they won't be able to attend to problems when they occur—and the longer one waits to intervene, the worse the problems will get. Insufficient staffing will also lead to a heightened sense of anxiety among your callers, particularly those who are mentally ill. If staff are overworked and hurried, they will likely become brusque or too busy to attend to callers' concerns.

An agency with staff that feels well-taken care of and protected is safer, by definition. Staff turnover is lower—callers have a reasonable expectation that they will reach a seasoned, well-trained professional. Finally, when staff have input into policies and procedures, callers' interests come first.

Respect Is a Matter of Safety

Integrity is perhaps the paramount human virtue. It is linked closely with another—dignity. It isn't only our own dignity that we must preserve. As professionals dealing with some of the most vulnerable members of our human family, people who are often shunned outcasts from both the larger society and, even more tragically, their own families, it is a moral responsibility that we strive to treat them with respect.

Respect, however, isn't something reserved solely for callers. Employees shouldn't experience any abuse from co-workers. A single incident, if it isn't too egregious can, in some circumstances, be considered an aberration. If you have absolute confidence that it won't ever reoccur, you can consider the incident closed. However, any repeat incident, any severe aggression, or any ongoing pattern of abuse or intimidation, should be discussed with supervisory personnel, human resources, or in some cases, law enforcement. Job ethics and professionalism radically diminish when there is a lack of respect.

Figure 57.1 Experience of One Veteran Dispatcher

One veteran dispatcher has described to me call-takers "setting-up" the dispatcher by not providing the full story on the incident, and police officers that are contemptuous or otherwise disrespectful to the dispatcher. Other police officers can cause disaster by mumbling into the microphone or not typing the entire message on their mobile device resulting in garbled or incomplete information.

Management must take action to address these issues. If not, at minimum, you will have a breakdown of morale. Worse, someone, citizen or emergency responder will be hurt or killed.

A final type of employee who can be profoundly destructive to morale is the person who is hostile to first responders and/or other staff at the call center. They seem to delight in causing conflict, although they would vehemently deny it.

This last type of employee is the most insidious. They devote a lot of time to creating both allies and dissension. Morale within an agency can plummet, and good employees sometimes quit just to get away from an increasingly nasty situation. To make matters worse, callers and first-responders are at increased risk, because call-takers, stressed or angered by the set-ups created by such a passive-aggressive manipulative co-worker can miss vital information. Because their aggressive behavior is covert rather than blatant, it is often very hard to get such an individual out of your agency. Nonetheless, supervisory staff should document every incident to establish that such an individual is acting in a way that puts both the public and emergency responders at risk.

Figure 57.2 One Veteran Supervisor's Account
As one veteran supervisor describes it:

"I have an employee like this, she is able to always say the right thing to get the other person to react in a negative way and suddenly she suddenly becomes the victim. She really gets enjoyment out of this. Yes, the other party reacts badly to her, but she sits back and can hardly wait for the other party to have to admit that they handled the situation wrong. She does the same thing to Law Enforcement Officers. She finds their trigger and reels them in, and then files a complaint against them for treating her wrong. On tape, she is accurate—they were out of line—but if you break down what she is doing, the whole thing is a set-up."

A Plan of Action

Safety planning must include the ideas of everyone who will need to be prepared: front line and relevant management staff. Don't forget people who may be around less than full time: volunteers, interns, and staff who work at multiple sites. A comprehensive plan should include:

- **A review of the current policies and procedures.** What policies are your staff expected to conform to that might contribute to an environment in which irritation, anger, or a sense of powerlessness is a natural consequence?
  a. **Are calls frequently dropped when people are put on hold?** Are they misdirected to the wrong number, requiring them to start over again?
  b. **An emphasis on consultation.** Consultation should include discussions regarding systemic safety concerns. This isn't a "venting" session – rather, it should be a planning session, in which you note dangerous issues affecting your agency: a caller's behavior, poor reporting of potentially dangerous individuals on the part of referring agencies, or poor coordination between call-takers and dispatchers. You will then establish action plans to make the particular situation safer.
  c. **Critical incidents.** Another form of consultation focuses on <u>critical incidents</u>. Whether a formal After Action Review (AAR), one-on-one with a supervisor, or more informal consultation with co-workers, dispatchers should attempt to understand problematic situations and see how they developed, and what turning points there were in the intervention. Consultation is an opportunity to get feedback, correction, and advice. Don't hesitate to use consultation due to either embarrassment or pride.
- **Inter-agency staffing.** Set up regular inter-agency staffing to discuss how better to interface with law enforcement, fire and emergency medical response, and, in many cases, the mental health system. Discuss problematic individuals who are causing a lot of attention within the overall systems (for example, an individual who makes chronic suicidal threats or para-suicidal actions). Have these agencies bring with them examples of the good, bad and ugly.

Figure 57.3 One Dispatcher's Experience

One dispatcher states: I have found that bringing the call center and emergency responders together serves a higher purpose. Rather than taking a call and sending it into the abyss, we get feedback beyond the times when go wrong.

- **Committees include administration and frontline personnel.** Committees should include both administration and front line personnel. Front line call-takers and dispatchers can identify the real problems or problem callers. The administrators are able to make decisions that effect change.
- **The 9-1-1 trainees should go on "ride-alongs" program with police, fire and EMS.** Trainees should go on "ride-alongs with other law enforcement personnel so that they can see and experience on the front lines the type of calls they will be handling.

Figure 57.4 Crisis Intervention Team/Training

One of the most exciting innovations in law enforcement is the CIT (Crisis Intervention Training/Team), in which law enforcement officers get 40 hours of training on dealing with mentally ill individuals in crisis. Many agencies have incorporated this model:

- Find out if your local law enforcement agency has a CIT team. If they do, ensure that all members of your dispatch center are familiar with its existence. If not, lobby to get such training made available.
- If there is a CIT team, always try to have your dispatchers access a CIT officer when there is a need for law enforcement to deal with an apparently mentally ill subject. You aren't guaranteed a response from a CIT officer—this depends on their availability at the time of the call. Nonetheless, if your jurisdiction has such a team, their specialized training would be an invaluable asset.

A Review of Critical Incidents

Consider some of the past aggressive or otherwise troubling interactions that have occurred between callers and dispatchers. Looking over past incidents is a helpful and necessary first step in learning to manage crises more effectively the next time around. Here are the things to note:

- What were the circumstances that led to the problem?
- What was the *first* sign that illustrated that the situation was getting volatile or problematic?
- Remember what they said and what they did.
- Consider what the call-taker's thoughts were at that time.
- Consider what the call-taker physically felt, at each stage of the encounter. This item may be the most important data you can recover. The sensations evoked within the context of an encounter with another person are physical expressions of intuition (Section II). When the call-taker next experiences those sensations, they are early warning signs that a similar situation is developing.

- What do you believe you might have done differently?
- Call-takers and dispatchers should be encouraged to ask their supervisor to review calls when a caller pushes their buttons. You can listen to the call to determine when the caller made you react so that you can plan a better response for the next incident.
- Dispatchers should be trained to recognize when they are "losing it," and about to say something unprofessional. When such a situation occurs, the dispatcher should tell the caller to hold, and then ask a co-worker, or their supervisor, to finish the call.

Figure 57.5 Experience of a Veteran Dispatcher

"I had a volunteer fire fighter's wife call because her grandchild was choking. She was abusive, demanding, and demeaning. I got so pissed off that I came very close to saying something I knew I would regret later. She was upset that it was taking so long, and didn't understand why I was asking all these questions. I told her that my questions were not delaying the response, that the aid crew has been dispatched, I told her, 'All I'm trying to do is help you help your grandchild by giving you some pre-arrival instructions to clear the airway.' But I felt like she was attacking my ability to do my job, and if her grandchild didn't survive it was a result of something I didn't provide. I can remember feeling hopeless—like there was something else I should be able to provide her to assure her we were doing everything we could do. If the outcome would have been negative I'm quite sure I would have second-guessed myself feeling like it was my failure that resulted in a bad outcome for her."

CHAPTER 58

A System-wide Response
to Problematic Callers

A Comprehensive Plan

Information must be shared among all those concerned with a problematic caller who interacts with multiple agencies. If they are presenting particular problems to the call-center, alert the responsible law enforcement agency of the need for an inter-agency consultation. Particularly concerning repeat callers who are mentally ill, this may include law enforcement, EMS, parole or probation officers, hospital administration, and mental health or substance-use treatment agencies. The best chance such callers have is when you function as a team on their behalf. All information, particularly regarding risk, must be shared, not only for ethical reasons, but also to ensure that such callers will be safe.

Information sharing isn't easy. Due to HIPA protections in the medical field, information is kept strictly confidential, unless the caller presents an immediate crisis. Nonetheless, state and federal laws allow medical and mental health information to be exchanged in emergent situations. As state statutes are different, your legal team should provide you with the relevant statutes that allow exchange of information in both emergent and non-emergent situations.

Splitting

Repeat callers can drain an enormous amount of energy and resources. They can also engender a lot of conflict within a call center (regarding what should be done with them) as well as between agencies. When there is a lot of conflict about a repeat caller—either within your dispatch center, or between the dispatch center and various other "players" in the system (crisis line, mental health agency, police, hospitals, etc.), consider splitting (Chapter 18).

- Compare notes on how the person presents to each person they have contact with in law enforcement, etc.
- Map out on paper the different "faces" they present.
- Map out on paper what strategies have been tried to deal with the person and what have been the results. Look for patterns, so that other people don't continue to try what has already failed.
- Develop a comprehensive plan to deal with the person, using outside consultation in really heated cases. Each part of the emergency response system as well as the mental health treatment system is assigned a role, and the proper way to play that role.
- Staff members within each agency must be informed of how to work with the person. They must sign off on a plan that requires them to deal with the caller in the agreed-upon way. No staff-member may undermine the plan by relating to the person differently. For example, if the person

has a ten minute limit on calls to the "crisis help line," and one "kind" volunteer feels sorry for them because they are crying, and lets them talk for two hours (it happens!!!!), the entire plan will be undermined and the person's splitting behaviors will increase exponentially.

Adult Protective Services

In addition to police and EMT, another resource to tap when dealing with elderly people is Adult Protective Services (APS). Your caller may be a "slow" risk due to their age and incompetence. It should be noted that APS in most states is over-worked, with too few social workers available. For this reason, it is conceivable that a high-risk case can slip through the cracks. After management makes a referral for APS follow-up regarding someone that the dispatch center repeatedly has to deal with, I recommend strongly that a summary of the referral be faxed to the agency. Such faxes are legal documents, and must be placed in the individual's file or should trigger the opening of a new file. This same referral process, including fax, should also accompany referrals to Child Protective Services.

Crying Wolf: Identifying and Helping Repetitive Callers and Abusers of Emergency Systems

Repeat Callers who are delusional. Delusional people sometimes get quite fixated on the police, or the emergency system. They deputize themselves, or call every night because "little people are in the walls and are scratching their way out." Every police department has at least one story of such an individual. Although typically harmless, they use up dispatchers' and law enforcement officers' energy. They are often desperate, but resistant to the very idea that they might need mental health treatment.

1. If the individual calls emergency dispatch, a response is legally required. Any apparently emergent call will, of course, require a response by law enforcement and/or emergency medical personnel.

2. Any repetitive non-emergent call to an emergency call center that is made by a delusional caller should require a follow-up to Adult Protective Services or the local mental health agency. This, of course, is the responsibility of 9-1-1 management to ensure that law enforcement follows-up on this issue, not the call-taker.

3. An inter-disciplinary team should be set up and a comprehensive response plan should be made to deal with the delusional individual more effectively. This should include:

   a. A committed attempt to enroll the person in mental health services. This shouldn't be discontinued after the first rejection. These individuals drain a tremendous amount of all-too-scarce funds from public coffers. It isn't only for the sake of the individual, but for the sake of the community that a concerted effort is made to direct them away from the emergency system.

   b. Alternative numbers to call, including a case manager, and/or a crisis line should be available so when the delusional person calls the emergency call center for non-emergent matters, operations management should, if possible, contact the crisis line or mental health services to follow up with the individual.

Chronically para-suicidal callers. These individuals either make a suicidal or self-mutilating gesture of varying degrees of severity or threaten suicide. Comprehensive case planning should include all agencies involved in the person's care (both acute and chronic) as well as those who *should* be involved in their care.

1. Injurious act:
   a. All face-to-face contacts should <u>minimize</u> any nurturing, comforting or sympathetic interactions. *NOTE: This can be in contradistinction to the response with a genuinely suicidal person. This section refers specifically to the repeat caller.*
   b. From dispatch personnel to law enforcement, paramedics, EMTs, mental health professionals and emergency room personnel, everyone should be matter-of-fact, as if patching up a leak in the basement wall. *This isn't meant as punitive, so no one should not be harsh: simply matter-of-fact.* The person should receive no emotional reinforcement for their actions.
   c. Comprehensive case planning should include how to reward the individual when they call a crisis line or after hours mental health services before making a suicidal attempt instead of calling 9-1-1 after an attempt. <u>To be clear, the rewards (emotional) involved are the responsibility of the treatment providers, not the emergency call center.</u>
   d. These cases can get remarkably contentious. It is sometimes best to get an expert, an outside consultant to assist the various members of the system in making an over-arching case plan that minimizes emotional rewards for self-mutilating behaviors.
2. Suicidal Threats, other "false alarm" calls:
   a. The first level of response is, again, to get the mental health system involved and make a case plan that will reward more functional behavior.
   b. If the person persists in false calling or otherwise ties up the emergency system, **PROSECUTE.** Depending on the caller's actions, during and subsequent to the call, there may be a number of possible charges, such as
      - Making a false or misleading statement to a public servant;
      - Obstructing a law enforcement officer;
      - Interference with a health care facility;
      - 9-1-1 abuse.

In some cases a municipality must pass an ordinance to enable prosecutors to charge the individual with a crime. I have seen considerable success through such prosecutions. Many people react that prosecuting someone who is mentally disturbed is cruel. On the contrary, it is kind. It is a mark of fundamental disrespect to not hold someone up to the standards of common decency and humanity. If we allow someone to act based exclusively on their own impulses, we say, in effect, "that's all you are good for." I have assisted in such plans even with individuals who are disabled developmentally or severely mentally ill and they have been escorted crying like heartbroken children to court and then to jail. Then, after spending some weeks in jail, they often stop calling. In short, their life improves greatly.

Figure 58.1 Experience of One Veteran Dispatcher
"We had a repeat caller who would call in about not having food, and eating cat food. He would call in false reports, but he thought they were real. No one would evaluate or incarcerate him until the city passed an ordinance prohibiting him from calling 9-1-1 when he didn't have an emergency. We had no recourse until the ordinance was passed, but subsequent to that he was prosecuted and his calls stopped."

Both these responses—the dispassionate attendance to the person who makes suicidal gestures, and the prosecution of the person who makes threats—should NOT be a decision made by one agency. There needs to be a frank discussion between the involved agencies. It must be understood that some individuals will "Up" their behaviors, becoming even more suicidal. Setting such limits is still the right thing to do.

It must be understood at the end of the discussion that these actions, rather than punitive, are for the sake of the caller as well as the community. The majority of repeat callers respond better when treated as people who have the capacity to change, and to cease acting in manipulative, attention-seeking ways.

Figure 58.2
Further discussion of this chapter is a subject of its own. The reader is welcome to contact the writer if they have a need for a consultation regarding the mental health side—not the legal aspects—of this type of problem.

For Repeat Callers With Psychological Problems: Those for Whom You Have Set Up a Plan of Action

The best way to manage repeat callers is to set up a comprehensive plan of action. Your call takers need their own plan, but sometimes the caller needs a plan as well, which call-takers will remind the caller, every time they call.

- Ensure that your call-takers have a protocol available to manage these repeat callers in non-emergent calls.
- Remind the caller of what they have been taught to do when feeling they are in psychological crisis. These can include walking away from what upsets them, deep calming breathing, or changing activities to get their minds on other things—whatever is in the plan.
- *"Remember the last time you...."* This can be used to remind someone of a past negative consequence to dissuade them from continuing or to remind them of a positive outcome, so that they remember how they succeeded in extricating themselves before.

APPENDIX:

Suggested Response Protocol for
9-1-1 Concerning Suspected
Excited Delirium Incidents

by Lt. Michael Paulus

Suggested Response Protocol for Suspected Excited Delirium Incidents

By Lt. Michael Paulus

NOTE: As discussed in detail in Chapter 52, Excited Delirium is a medical syndrome that is included within a general category: Chaotic Rage. It should not be incumbent upon the 9-1-1 call-taker, eyewitnesses or first responders to distinguish between excited delirium and other similar, possibly less dangerous forms of chaotic rage. Therefore, the protocols below are generally applicable, whatever the cause.

When considering a response to suspected Excited Delirium incidents, it is important to understand what the law enforcement/correction officer is facing. Dr. Deborah Mash of the University of Miami Brain Endowment Center has called Excited Delirium, "a medical emergency that presents itself as a law enforcement problem."

Keeping this in mind, it is comparable to dispatching the fire department to a bank robbery. They do not have the appropriate equipment or training to handle the high risk nature of a bank robbery. By the same token, EMS personnel are not dispatched to intervene in domestic disputes.

Why, then, is law enforcement or corrections sent to a medical emergency that requires a minimum of an advanced life support ambulance crew to address? There is nothing on the officer's duty belt, in their squad car, or in their facility that will address the hyperthermia, the acidosis, the cardiovascular collapse, or other life-threatening issues that are common in an Excited Delirium incident.

Dr. Michael Curtis, of St. Michael's Hospital in Steven's Point, Wisconsin has said, in reference to Excited Delirium, "The legal issues can wait, the life-threatening medical emergency will not." The problem is that unless the individual is under complete physical control, medical assistance cannot be rendered. For this reason, law enforcement personnel must get the right resources to the scene as quickly as possible to give the subject the best possibility of surviving. For this to occur, it is necessary to develop a multi-disciplinary approach to this multi-faceted problem.

Some of the most common stakeholders that need to be a part of this multi-disciplinary approach include: law enforcement/corrections, EMS personnel, fire personnel, 9-1-1 call-takers and dispatchers, emergency room physicians/nurses, coroners, medical examiners, mental health professionals/consumers, agency risk managers, and the appropriate State/District attorney. Your jurisdiction may have different stakeholders, maybe more or maybe less, but the critical issue is to identify those that are, or should be, a part of a best-practices response to these, all too often, fatal incidents.

Once the stakeholders are identified, decision-makers from each will need to discuss their role in the proposed protocol, and an agreement must be reached as to how these incidents are to be handled in the future. This should be documented in the form of a policy/protocol depending on the methods common to each resource.

What is offered here is a successful multi-jurisdictional response that has been in place since July 1, 2008 in Champaign County, Illinois.[12] This can be used as a template for your community to help gather the various interested parties to the table to create a protocol that works for you within the confines of the resources you have available.

The effectiveness of this protocol relies upon the 9-1-1 telecommunicator (TC) to recognize the caller's report as describing agitated chaotic behaviors that represent possible excited delirium, and to be able to elicit enough information to make a determination if additional resources are needed at the scene. This would include a law enforcement response along with an EMS/Fire Rescue response dispatched at the same time.

For example, when the TC receives a call from a citizen about someone "acting bizarre", "just flipped out", "running in the cold with no clothes on", he or she should begin to gather additional information on the subject. There are warning signs that are useful in determining if the enhanced response protocol is warranted, such as:

- Is there a history of stimulant drug use/abuse?
- Is there a history of mental illness, particularly schizophrenia?
- Did this behavior occur suddenly without warning?
- Is the subject screaming, yelling, or making grunting or animal sounds?
- Is the person inappropriately clothed for the situation?
- Is the person sweating profusely?
- Is the person exhibiting superhuman strength, seemingly unlimited endurance, or impervious to pain?

These questions are not all-inclusive, but they can give the TC and the responding units vital information on what it is they are responding to before they get there. The TC should remain on the line with the caller until the responders arrive on the scene to take over.

It is important to understand that neither the dispatcher, the officers, or the EMS personnel are "diagnosing" what is causing the subject's behavior. It could be the result of stimulant drug abuse/overdose, a head injury, thyroid issues, hyperthermia, or autism, to name a few. Neither the TC nor the first responders should get "fixated" on a reason for the medical emergency. It is of utmost importance to understand that these questions can only be answered in the Emergency Room.

The number of personnel sent to the scene will be dependant on what resources are available, but four to six (4-6) law enforcement personnel should be dispatched to the scene. Interagency agreements are common to allow various departments to share resources in times of emergency. These incidents are an exemplar of the kind of emergency that requires enough personnel to get control of the subject and on the way to the hospital as soon as possible.

EMS should be sent at the same time as law enforcement personnel. This will save precious time in getting the medical personnel and equipment to the scene as quickly as possible. Some communities have a combined EMS/Fire Department. Those that don't will then need to consider if sending a Fire Rescue truck is a possibility along with EMS. Some jurisdictions have as part of their City Ordinance that any "medical emergency" requires a Fire Rescue truck be sent. If this is the case, the EMS crew as well as the Fire Rescue personnel should be dispatched to the scene. The role of the Fire Rescue will be discussed shortly.

One of the issues with a suspected Excited Delirium response is that, currently, there is no emergency medical dispatch (EMD) card for the TC to refer to when it happens. The need, then, is for the 9-1-1 administrators to create a dual response card or computer-aided dispatch (CAD) ticket. Our local 9-1-1 manager created a dual response ticket by entering the code "EXCITC" into the dispatch program. This created a law enforcement ticket that prompted the TC to send four to six officers. If the primary agency does not have enough officers available, they will be dispatched from neighboring jurisdictions. There was also an EMS ticket that dispatched an advanced life support ambulance (ALS) and a Fire Rescue truck within our city.

The law enforcement response should ideally include a Crisis Intervention Team (CIT) officer, an officer with a less lethal weapon, and a supervisor. The role of the Fire Rescue personnel, usually three to five firemen, is to support EMS by either assisting the paramedic in the back of the ambulance or driving the ambulance to the hospital. They should respond "no code" and park in a location as to not block in the ambulance or responding units. If the Fire Rescue is the EMS response, then they should respond as a primary first responder with lights and siren.

If multiple jurisdictions are dispatched to the scene, including EMS and/or Fire Rescue, it is wise to send all of the responding units to their own radio channel. The reason for this is so they can communicate with each other; advising on the current location of the subject, the best route to the scene, or safety considerations at the scene, instead of having to relay that through the dispatch center and then on to the responding units. This is dependant on the jurisdiction being able to communicate with surrounding agencies/resources. Unfortunately, this is not always the case and the TC may end up being tasked with passing information from one resource to the next.

It is generally better for law enforcement to delay making physical contact with the subject until EMS/ Fire Rescue has arrived on the scene. This decision is balanced by the safety of the first responders, witnesses, and bystanders on one side and the safety of the subject themselves on the other. No two situations are exactly the same: the situation will dictate the tactics the responders will use. This is why sending EMS/Fire Rescue at the same time as law enforcement/corrections is critical to getting the necessary medical services to the scene as quickly as possible.

The EMS unit will need to stage closer to the subject than is usual in many other situations; this is not to say they should put themselves in needless jeopardy. It is, of course, incumbent upon the law enforcement personnel to keep the EMS personnel safe, as they do not have the means to protect themselves from serious injury should the subject attack.

The TC should advise the responding law enforcement units where the EMS unit will respond to unless law enforcement advises differently. In a multi-jurisdictional response protocol, the EMS personnel are the ones who have the training and resources to deal with the medical emergency. It is therefore critical that they be in a position to see the subject as soon as possible. If there is a field sedation protocol in place, it will be important for them to observe the subject to estimate the amount of medication needed or at the very least to call in to the Emergency Room to get orders from the attending physician.

Careful documentation of the information received by the TC is critical for a complete report after the fact, whether the subject survives or not. Information on when the behaviors began *before* the first responders arrived is imperative for investigators to complete an accurate picture of the actions of the officers and EMS personnel. This information can assist in determining the effectiveness of the response protocol and what, if any, changes need to be made.

If the subject dies, there most certainly will be a thorough investigation. However, if the subject does not die, the opportunity is usually missed for further investigation. The incident may be memorialized in a station house story about the "naked guy out in the snow bank". This loses a valuable opportunity to document what Dr. Mash has called "flicker events" in which a person gets into this excited state and then works their way out of it. These flicker events could be predictors of future incidents that portend a dire ending.

The TC may have access to information about the subject showing a history of similar incidents in the past. The dispatch center should "flag" a person with an alert that articulates previous contact with the subject of a violent nature requiring the multi-disciplinary response.

The investigator and administrator should understand that it is usually after the subject has already reached an out of control state that the call goes out for assistance. So law enforcement is already behind the curve on this subject's condition. This process of the sudden unexpected in-custody death has been likened to a "freight train to death". If law enforcement are called and arrive on scene with a subject who is already "pulling in to the station"; it may be that they have been dispatched to just observe the person's demise. Unfortunately, the person may have reached the tipping point in which their physical condition is irreversible. The TC and the officers are then left with questions, wondering what happened and what they could have done differently.

If the investigation focuses on just what the officers did and not the condition of the subject, the potential for inaccurate conclusions are possible. This will not help the family of the subject, the TC, the officers involved, the agency, or the community to process the incident. This is why it is vitally important for the TC to collect as much relevant information as possible to share with the first responders as well as investigators later.

To summarize, dispatch personnel should gain as much information from the caller on the condition of the subject as possible, and begin to realize that this may be medical emergency, and dispatch enough (4-6) officers/correctional personnel as well as an Advanced Life Support (ALS) ambulance to the scene together.

Follow up questions, if possible, with the caller will provide valuable information to the first responders on the nature of the subject's behavior as well as how long it has been going on. The call taker should attempt to obtain information on any substance abuse (particularly stimulant drugs) as well as any history of mental illness or noncompliance with mental health medication. This is the minimum needed by first responders. Information regarding profuse sweating, demonstrating superhuman strength, attraction to glass, screaming for no apparent reason, or hallucinations are just a few of the clues to responders that this could be an Excited Delirium incident.

It is important to understand that this incident may start out as a "routine" medical call and once EMS is on the scene, they may call out the possible Excited Delirium response, which would require additional law enforcement officers to be dispatched.

When a TC sends out the call of a "suspected/possible Excited Delirium" incident, they are not making a diagnosis. What they are doing is implementing a protocol that has policies and procedures in place to send multiple resources to a medical emergency. If it turns out that the subject was not in the throes of Excited Delirium, then the unneeded resources are sent back to their respective station houses.

Call-takers/dispatchers should realize that law enforcement is very dependant upon the dispatcher's information in these incidents. Officers on the ground trust that the TC has the information and insights necessary for a successful resolution. The TC should understand that if the incident fits the criteria for dispatching the extra resources, they should dispatch those resources as soon as possible. As with any new protocol, there will surely be calls about individuals who turn out not to be Excited Delirium subjects. There will be a learning curve as the dispatchers gets better at filtering the information and getting the right resources to the scene.

This guide may be used as a template to develop your multi-disciplinary response to this multi-faceted problem based on the resources available in your community.

If you have questions about this protocol, or would like a sample policy, please contact Lt. Michael Paulus at michael923@yahoo.com or at (217) 202-4232.

Endnotes

1   This checklist conceivably could be adapted in training to help new dispatchers prepare for the emotional challenges of the work.

2   One of the best books on manipulation, one where I learned a lot of the information described above is: Allen, B. & Bosta, D. (1981-2002). *Games Criminals Play: How you can profit by knowing them?* Berkeley: Rae John Publishers. (ISBN: 0-9605226-0-3).

3   I am grateful to the late Dan Kelleher, former professor of Antioch University, for the image of the "undamaged self."

4   Kris Mohandie, J. Reid Meloy, Ph.D., A.B.P.P., & Peter I. Collins, M.C.A., M.D., F.R.C.P., "Suicide by Cop Among Officer-Involved Shooting Cases," *Journal of Forensic Sciences, 54*(2), 456-462. Retrieved February 11, 2009.

5   Levinas, Emanuel. (1985). *Ethics and infinity: Conversations with Philip Nemo* (Richard Cohen, Trans.). Pgh, PA: Duquesne University.

6   de Becker, Gavin. (1997). *The gift of fear: Survival signals that protect us from violence.* United States and Canada: Little Brown and (1999) *Protecting the gift: Keeping children and teenagers safe (and parents sane).* New York: Random House.

7   Edgerton, Robert B. (1992). *Sick societies: Challenging the myth of primitive harmony.* New York: The Free Press.

8   This method is also called "active listening" or "mirroring." However, mirroring often entails repeating word-for-word what the other person is saying. This can easily be experienced as taunting on mocking. As for active listening, this term often carries a certain ideological baggage—through active listening, many counselors try to establish a "holding," nurturing relationship with a client, thereby either making them "feel better," or in the safety of such "validation," allowing them to emote freely. This is, in a subtle way, manipulative. By talking to another person as if they are fragile, they may feel so, or they may feel that you are *trying* to make them feel fragile. In either event, this can encourage the person to become more childish, angrier or even enraged. Paraphrasing, on the other hand, simply establishes that you are truly listening and have understood what they have said.

9   I am indebted to John Holttum, MD, Child Psychiatrist from Tacoma, Washington. I attended a presentation given by Dr. Holttum which greatly influenced me in terms of how to "subdivide" the presenting behaviors of youth and how best to intervene with them. I must underscore that any intervention recommendations are mine, and may be at variance to those Dr. Holttum might offer.

10 The subject of impulsive youth, often diagnosed with ADD/ADHD, deserves more controversy than it is currently receiving in both media and clinical sources. I strongly recommend that everyone concerned with youth read two contrarian books, one by Louv, Richard. (2005). *Last child in the woods: Saving our children from nature-deficit disorder.* Chapel Hill, NC: Algonquin Books. The other book by Sax, Leonard (2007). *Boys adrift: The five factors driving the growing epidemic of unmotivated boys and underachieving young men.* Philadelphia: Basic Books. Whether you end up agreeing with all of what either of the authors proposes, they will require you to think afresh about this subject. And in an era where medications are slung like bon-bons at children, often with little clinical assessment or sound treatment, this is absolutely necessary.

11 I owe a debt for some of the basic information in this section to a form of training called Professional Assault Response Training (PART), thanks to a workshop I attended approximately 20 years ago. I have made major changes in their basic four-part schema, as well as adding a significant amount of new data. Therefore, my approach is, in many aspects, quite different, and it shouldn't be confused with their procedures.

12 The American College of Emergency Physicians (ACEP) put out a white paper in September of 2009 expressing the ideas that were already in place in Champaign County almost a year prior.

ABOUT THE AUTHOR

Ellis Amdur

Edgework founder Ellis Amdur received his B.A. in psychology from Yale University in 1974 and his M.A. in psychology from Seattle University in 1990. He is both a National Certified Counselor and a State Certified Child Mental Health Specialist. He has written a number of books concerning communication with mentally ill and emotionally disturbed individuals and the de-escalation of aggression, all of which are available through www.edgework.info.

Since the late 1960s, Amdur has trained in various martial arts systems, spending 13 of these years studying in Japan. He is a recognized expert in classical and modern Japanese martial traditions and has also authored three iconoclastic books, and one DVD on martial arts subjects.

Since his return to America in 1988, Ellis Amdur has worked in the field of crisis intervention. He has developed a range of training and consultation services, as well as a unique style of assessment and psychotherapy. These are based on a combination of phenomenological psychology and the underlying philosophical premises of classical Japanese martial traditions. Amdur's professional philosophy can best be summed up in this idea: the development of an individual's integrity and dignity is the paramount virtue. This can only occur when people live courageously, regardless of the circumstances, and take responsibility for their roles in making the changes they desire.

Ellis Amdur is a dynamic public speaker and trainer who presents his work throughout the United States and internationally. He is noted for his sometimes outrageous humor as well as his profound breadth of knowledge. His vivid descriptions of aggressive and mentally ill people and his true-to-life role-playing of the behaviors in question give participants an almost first-hand experience of facing the real individuals in question.

Check out www.edgework.info
- to read more about Ellis Amdur's work;
- to purchase his books on de-escalation of aggression;
- and to secure his services, either for on-site training or consultation.

www.ingramcontent.com/pod-product-compliance
Lightning Source LLC
Chambersburg PA
CBHW061757260326
41914CB00006B/1144